Insights

Kim

LATIN AMERICA

Thomas Orin Flickema

Paul W. Kane

CHARLES E. MERRILL PUBLISHING CO.
A Bell & Howell Company
Columbus, Ohio

Toronto • London • Sydney

A MERRILL SOCIAL STUDIES PROGRAM

GLOBAL INSIGHTS: PEOPLE AND CULTURES

China

India

Latin America

Middle East

Soviet Union

Sub-Saharan Africa

**Teacher's Guide for Global Insights:
People and Cultures**

**Evaluation Program for Global Insights:
People and Cultures (spirit duplicating masters)**

ISBN 0-675-01911-7
Published by
CHARLES E. MERRILL PUBLISHING CO.
A Bell & Howell Company
Columbus, Ohio 43216

AUTHORS

Thomas Orin Flickema is Dean of the Graduate School at Kearney State College in Kearney, Nebraska. Formerly, he was Chairman of the History Department at California State University, Fullerton, and the Director of Latin American Studies. He is co-author of a book on sixteenth-century Peru. He also is the author of several articles on historical research and has written reviews for *The Hispanic American Historical Review* and *The Americas*. Flickema has read several papers at historical meetings and serves on the Board of Governors of the Orange County Area Social Science Association. He is a member of the Hispanic-American Historical Association and the Conference on Latin American History.

Paul W. Kane is a Professor of Education and Acting Dean of the School of Human Development and Community Service at California State University, Fullerton, where he was formerly the Chairman of the Division of Teacher Education. He is the author of various articles, some of which have appeared in *Social Education* and *The Social Studies*. Kane was a member of the California Social Science Framework Committee and has participated in conferences of the National Council for the Social Studies. He is active in the California Council for Social Studies and Phi Delta Kappa.

EDITORIAL STAFF

Myra Immell, Rosemarie Trenjan, Cheryl Currutt, Ann Weiland

ART STAFF

Project Artist: Katie White
Art Director: Lester Shumaker
Cover Design: Larry Koons
Artists: Joan Moor, Dave Gossell
Unit Map: Laurel Casazza
Text Maps: June Barnes

PHOTO STAFF

Susan Marquart

REVIEWERS

Dr. Susanne Cannan
Director of Social Studies
City School District of Buffalo
Buffalo, New York

Dr. Marie Edwards
Supervisor of Social Studies and Foreign Languages
Gary, Indiana

Dr. Dana Kurfman
Social Studies Supervisor
Prince George's Public Schools
Upper Marlboro, Maryland

Tom Leidich
Supervisor of Social Studies
Columbus Public Schools
Columbus, Ohio

Dr. Dorothy Scott
Director of Secondary Instruction
Tyler Independent School District
Tyler, Texas

Dr. Albert A. Seretny
Director of Instruction
Greater New Haven State Technical College
Hamden, Connecticut

PREFACE

LATIN AMERICA. Those countries of South America where French, Portuguese, or Spanish is the spoken language, including roughly all countries of the U.S.A. border with Mexico, but excluding parts of the West Indies. Spanish is the dominating language, although the language of the largest country, Brazil, is Portuguese.

If you were to look up the name Latin America in the *Statesman's Year-Book,* you would find the above description of that area. Nothing is said about the human element, about the people. Who are those people? How do they live? In what do they believe? Where did their civilization begin? What events in their history have shaped their way of life?

This text provides the answers to these questions as well as to many others. It introduces you to the people of Latin America, to their land, and to their history in a straightforward, easy-to-read format. The text offers objective factual information that allows you to arrive at your own conclusions about the countries of Latin America and the Latin American people. The intent of the text is to present the Latin Americans as Latin Americans, not as Latin Americans viewed through the eyes of their North American neighbors.

Each of the eleven chapters of *Insights: Latin America* opens with a colorful photo and two overview questions which alert you to the chapter theme. A primary source reading and a short paragraph which involve you in the chapter topic follow. Next is the background narrative, which is interspersed with primary source readings and thought-provoking questions designed to provide the basic information needed to know and understand a culture. A Case Study then focuses on a particular event, incident, or factor that supplements the basic understanding of the chapter theme. In the Exploration, the last section of each chapter, you have an opportunity to put the topic into perspective, to see how the topic fits into the overall picture of Latin America and its people.

John Paxton, *The Statesman's Year-Book: World Gazetteer* (New York: St. Martin's Press, 1975), p. 336.

Because the written word alone does not always result in a three-dimensional view, photographs, maps, charts, and other illustrations appear throughout the text. These provide visual reinforcement of the written material by giving you an opportunity to see what you have been reading about. All of the above factors combined do more than "teach" about the Latin American culture. They work together to give you a feel for the people, their way of life, and the problems which confront them.

In today's world, it is important for all of us to have some insight into the modes and manners of all our global neighbors, especially those who live so very near to us. It is not enough to read the newspaper headlines and watch short television film clips, for they relate only part of the story. A great many Latin Americans have immigrated to—and settled in—the United States. In their efforts to make a home and life for themselves here, they have had to learn our language and our culture. It is to our advantage to learn about—and try to understand—their heritage, their land, and their customs. This text will help you to do that by doing what its title implies—provide insight into the very essence of the Latin American people.

Insights

LATIN AMERICA

Thomas Orin Flickema, Paul W. Kane

ATLANTIC

OCEAN

Table of Contents

1	The Vast Environment	4
2	The Human Diversity	18
3	At the Root of Living	28
4	A View of Life	40
5	The Sword and the Cross	50
6	The Need to Learn	60
7	Growth and Urbanization	70
8	The Land of the Campesino	80
9	A Political Tradition	92
10	The Marxist Way	104
11	The New Politics: A Time for Change	116
	Glossary	129
	Index	132

What is meant by the "environmental variety of Latin America"?

In what ways does the environment influence the way of life of the Latin American people?

The Vast Environment

The motor purred and sang. Santiago [Chile] shrank rapidly
away. . . . At our side stood a solid wall that seemed to grow higher
as we rose—the western side of the Andes.

Five, six, seven thousand feet and we turned eastward over the
broad valley of the Juncal River and toward the mountains. We
gained on them. At first they looked like colossal gobs of
sponge-cake sprinkled with a thin coating of powdered sugar. In
another moment they were beneath us, or I thought so. . . . The
great gobs of sponge cake were not the Andes at all. They were only
the foothills of the Andes. We hadn't started to climb. . . .

The poppies and hayfields gave way to jagged, contorted cliffs
and rocks, around and over which wound and twisted the
Aconcagua River. . . . All the time we were climbing up, up,
up—eight thousand feet, nine, ten—two miles. The sponge cake
became a coconut cake. It was all solid white, completely iced over.
This, I thought, is the Andes proper. But as I looked ahead a wall
loomed still higher, so high that it seemed to have no top. Then I
realized that these were just the foothills of the Andes.

. . . We were still climbing. I glanced at the altimeter; fourteen
thousand feet, then presently fifteen thousand, sixteen, seventeen,
eighteen thousand. . . . there, between two ridges, was a giant icy
mirror with crags and peaks reflected in its glacial blue waters, the
Laguna del Inca or Inca Lake. . . .

Up and up, nineteen, twenty thousand feet, twenty-one
thousand, twenty-one thousand five hundred feet. What an
altitude! . . .

. . . It was like going to heaven in an airplane. We were just
above the cordillera, the central range of the mighty mountains.
Beneath us, jagged peaks . . . seemed to reach up threateningly. All
around were countless slender snowy peaks. To the north the
granddaddy of them all . . . Aconcagua, 23,083 feet high, looked
calmly and silently down upon the whole continent. To the south,
Aconcagua's companion, Tupungato, only a hundred feet lower.
Two giant sentinels [guards] of this fantastic garden of the gods.

Edward Tomlinson, *The Other Americans: Our Neighbors to the South*
(New York: Charles Scribner's Sons, 1943), pp. 309–312.

As we cleared the western edge of the central range and hung . . . between these two magnificent peaks, the morning sun splashed its first yellow rays over the mountains, and the great white world became a solid mass of glittering gold. Then it changed. It became a mass of shimmering silver. The rearing peaks looked like great foaming bubbles. I looked south at Tupungato, then north to Aconcagua. They wore crowns of sparkling diamonds, so bright from the light of old Sol [the sun] that it hurt my eyes to look.

Most visitors to Latin America are like the airplane passenger who wrote about this flight over the Andes. They cannot believe the beauty and grandeur of the mountains. But the vast geography of Latin America is more than just lofty mountains. There are low-lying inland and coastal plains, fertile valleys, great river systems, tropical jungles, and parched deserts. There is a wide range of climates. The rivers and rainfall give some areas a lot of water while others have little or none. Three fourths of the mountainous region is in the equatorial zone. Yet most Latin Americans live in temperate or cool climates. This varied environment makes Latin America a complex land that greatly influences the way the people live and what they expect out of life.

Earthquakes are common in Latin America. Damage may range from the loss of a few buildings, as seen here, to the destruction of almost an entire city.

Fred Ward for Black Star

BACKGROUND

Huge mountain ranges dominate the Latin American environment. One of these is the Andes. The longest continuous mountain chain in the world, the Andes Mountains stretch four thousand miles, from northern Colombia and Venezuela to the tip of South America. But these mountains have created problems. One is that they block communications. Most of the people who live in the mountains are in scattered, lonely villages. Since travel in the Andes is so difficult, the villagers have very little contact with other areas. For this reason, their loyalties and ties are to their region rather than to their nation. There has been talk about developing more and better transportation systems in the mountains. But since most of the passes in the Andes are over ten thousand feet above sea level, construction work is hard, costs a lot, and takes time.

Another problem is that the mountains are geologically young. For this reason, there are often volcanic eruptions, avalanches, earthquakes, and seaquakes (underwater earthquakes). They cause tidal waves that can damage and even level towns on the coast. Yet, the earthquakes are worse. In the following newspaper report, two American missionaries give their account of an earthquake in Peru.

> It was a quiet Sunday afternoon in Caraz.
>
> Michael Boyd Nielsen . . . and Allen Anthony Arvig . . . were sitting in a . . . plastered adobe building used as a chapel. . . .
>
> "The building started shaking. I didn't know what had happened. I jumped up," Mike said. "The shaking continued and we ran downstairs to the patio as plaster started falling. We stayed in the patio until the shaking stopped.
>
> "The first thing I noticed besides the dust and the dirt . . . [was] the screams of the women and the cries of the babies . . ." Mike said.
>
> Allen said: "The thing I remember most was trying to run up the street. We could hardly make it because of all the fallen walls. The people were worried that Paron Lake above town had broken and this meant the whole city would be wiped out. Everyone started rushing toward the mountains. Everyone believed the whole city would be flooded immediately. . . ."
>
> Said Allen: "It's really a strange feeling to know a city so well and see it completely destroyed. . . .
>
> "Very few people worried about the injured. The doctors were up in the mountains with their families. The hospital was completely caved in. . . ."
>
> "It's hard to say how many got killed," Mike said.

Martin P. Houseman, "Mormon Missionaries Tell of Andean Quake Horror," *Independent Press-Telegram* (Long Beach, California), June 6, 1970, p. A–4. UPI article.

Still, people are drawn to the mountains. Some come to mine the rich deposits of copper, iron, silver, tin, lead, and other minerals. Others come to grow grain and coffee or to raise livestock in the rich soil of the valleys and plateaus between the mountains. In these cool and fertile regions rose the great Indian civilizations of Mexico and Peru. And, even today, these areas are among the most important and most heavily populated in Latin America.

What draws people to the mountains? Would you like to live there? Why or why not?

How have the mountains in Latin America been a barrier to progress? How might they contribute toward future development?

The Argentine *pampas* are vast, temperate plains good for raising cattle and grain. Very few people live in certain undeveloped areas of the *pampas*.

Thomas Flickema

The Venezuelan *llanos* are not as vast as the *pampas* of Argentina but are like them in some ways. Iron ore deposits in the *llano* have led to development of this region.

Cornell Capa for Magnum

The Plains . . . Coastal plains, seldom more than fifty miles wide, extend along the coast of Mexico, through the Yucatán Peninsula, and into Guatemala, Honduras, and Nicaragua. In addition to these, there are the broad inland plains spread over southern Brazil, Paraguay, Uruguay, Argentina, Venezuela, and Colombia. Two of the most interesting of these plains are the *pampas* of Argentina and the *llanos* of Colombia and Venezuela.

The *pampas* extend almost four hundred miles to the north, west, and south of Buenos Aires. One American traveler described them this way:

> . . . a flight over the flat plains to the city of Buenos Aires becomes a monotonous stretch of green, rolling away in uneven rectangles and triangles between streaks of brown roads. Yet that stretch of green is the lifeblood of the nation: thousands of acres of wheat, rich pastures, an endless garden intensively cultivated.
>
> The broad level grassy *pampa* is a glorified Iowa or a second Texas. . . . cattle, . . . sheep, . . . acres of agricultural land! The figures are stupefying. There they are beneath the plane, vast fields that extend for miles on end. Cattle, horses, sheep, thousands of rhea—the South American ostrich. Rich lands like the delta lands of the Mississippi, something like the Iowa corn country, a little like the prairie lands of northern Illinois and northern Indiana, a little more like Texas.

Until the late 1800's, the most important person on the *pampas* was the *gaucho*, the man who worked the cattle that roamed the vast area.

Edward Tomlinson, *The Other Americans: Our Neighbors to the South* (New York: Charles Scribner's Sons, 1943), pp. 321–322.

Isabelle Havre/Organization of American States

The Argentine *gaucho* had much in common with the North American cowboy of the old West. The *gaucho's* nomadic way of life came to an end as civilization advanced.

Argentine author Domingo Sarmiento describes the life of the *gaucho* and his family:

In the absence of all the means of civilization and progress, the education of the people is as follows: The women look after the house, get the meals ready, shear the sheep, milk the cows, make the cheese, and weave the cloth used for clothes. All domestic jobs are done by women; on them rests the burden of all the labor. The boys exercise their strength and have their fun by gaining skill in the use of the lasso and the bolas [three leather thongs tied together, each with a rock or steel ball tied to the end]. When they can ride, which is as soon as they have learned to walk, they do some small services on horseback. When they become stronger, they race over the country on their horses. On reaching puberty, they take to breaking wild colts. With early manhood comes complete independence and idleness.

Country life, then, has developed all the physical but none of the intellectual powers of the gaucho. The gaucho does not labor; he finds his food and clothing ready to his hand. If he is an owner, his own flocks give him both. If he owns nothing himself, he finds them in the house of someone else. The necessary care of the herds is reduced to short trips and pleasure parties; the branding is a festival, the arrival of which is received with joy. Branding is something which draws all the men from sixty miles around, and gives them the chance to show off incredible skill with the lasso. The gaucho arrives at the spot on his best horse, riding at a slow and measured pace; he halts at a little distance and puts his leg over his horse's neck to enjoy the sight leisurely. If he feels like it, he slowly gets off his horse, uncoils his lasso, and flings it at some bull, passing like a flash of lightning forty paces from him; he catches him by one hoof, as he intended, and quietly coils his leather cord again.

By the late 1800's, civilization had reached the *pampas* in the form of railroads, immigrants, and farming. The *gaucho*, and the *gaucho* way of life, began to disappear. Today the *pampas* cover about 20 percent of Argentina. They house two out of three Argentines. They hold 70 percent of the nation's railroads. More than half of Argentina's cattle, and almost all of its flax, wheat, and corn, come from the *pampas*.

The other great plains area of Latin America, the *llanos*, stretches from the delta of the Orinoco River in Venezuela westward into southern Colombia. The areas along the rivers are level, but the rest is rolling plains and low mesas—broad, flat, elevated areas. Cattle raising has been the main economic activity of the *llanos* since the sixteenth century. But, because of

Adapted from Domingo Faustino Sarmiento, *Life in the Argentine Republic in the Days of the Tyrants, or Civilization and Barbarism* (New York: Collier Books, 1961), pp. 37–39. Foreword by Eugenio Villicana. (Foreword: © Macmillan Publishing Co., Inc., 1962).

the climate, the cattle industry is not what it could be. In the novel *Doña Barbara*, author Rómulo Gallegos tells how the weather affects the life on the *llanos*.

It rained, and rained, and rained. For days nothing else happened. The cattlemen who had been outside their houses had returned to them, for the creeks and streams would flow over into the prairie and there would soon be no path to use. Nor any need to use one.

The marsh was full to overflowing, for the winter had set in with a will. One day the black snout of a crocodile rose to the surface, and soon there would be alligators too, for the creeks were filling fast and they could travel all over the prairie.

Rain, rain, rain! The creeks had flowed over and the pools were full. The people began to fall ill, struck down by malaria, shivering with cold, their teeth chattering. They became pale, and then green, and crosses began to spring up in the Altamira cemetery.

But the rivers began to go down at last, and the ponds on the river banks to dry up; the alligators began to abandon the creeks, to gorge themselves on the Altamira cattle. The fever was dying out.

The drought had begun to hold sway. It was now the time for driving to the water holes the cattle who had never known them, or had forgotten them in the agony of thirst. The rutted beds of creeks long dried up ran here and there through the brownish weeds. In some marshes there still remained a little oozy, warm water in which rotting steers, who, crazy with thirst, had leaped into the deepest part of the holes and there, swollen with too much drinking, had been trapped and had died. Great bands of buzzards wheeled above the pools. Death is a pendulum swinging over the Plain, from flood to drought and from drought to flood.

In recent years, a dam has been built across the Guárico River to protect against floods and to irrigate the *llanos*. Thousands of acres which once were wasteland during the dry season are now fertile, watered pasture.

What and where are the *pampas* and the *llanos*?

What is produced on the *pampas*? On the *llanos*?

What was the life style of the nineteenth-century *gaucho*? Why did his life style change? In what ways did it change?

How do you think life on the *pampas* compares with that on the *llanos*?

Adapted from Rómulo Gallegos, *Doña Barbara*, trans. Robert Malloy (New York: Peter Smith, 1931), pp. 291–294, 432–433.

Rivers and Deserts . . . Latin America has five great river systems: the Cauca-Magdalena in Colombia, the Orinoco in Venezuela, the Amazon and the São Francisco in Brazil, and the Paraná-La Plata system in the southern part of the continent. One of the largest rivers is the Amazon, which stretches nearly four thousand miles across South America. Its immensity is described below.

Brazilians, of course, can . . . boast that the Amazon is the greatest river on this planet. Curiously, it took man a long time to get around to measuring it exactly. Not until he had orbited the earth in outer space did scientists—in 1963—record the dimensions of this mammoth "river sea." They discovered that it is even bigger than anyone expected.

Collecting water from thousands of tributaries, the Amazon dumps enough of it into the South Atlantic every day to cover the whole state of Texas to a depth of more than an inch. Along with all the water, billions of tons of soil, salts, and sediments are flushed into the sea. Yet the water of one of the main tributaries, the Rio Negro, is as chemically pure as distilled water.

Three hundred feet deep in places, the Amazon is the longest navigable river in the world. Ocean-going vessels regularly follow its meandering path through the center of the continent two thousand miles upstream to Iquitos, Peru.

The mighty Amazon River is the longest in the world. It drains an area that is two-thirds as large as the continental United States. Although the river has many possible uses, there are many problems in developing it.

Loren McIntyre/Woodfin Camp, Inc.

As one author phrased it, "The Amazon is usually considered more hostile than homey." The Amazon does have over 2 million square miles of river basin which a combination of heavy rainfall and heat have made the largest equatorial forest, or jungle, in the world. The very high humidity and

Reprinted by permission of the Publisher, Thomas Nelson, Inc. From the book *Brazil, Awakening Giant*, p. 38. Copyright © 1967 by Kathleen Seegers.

Manaus is a large, busy city in the Brazilian jungle about one thousand miles from the mouth of the Amazon River. Pictured is a colorful riverside market run by people of the area. It is just a few blocks from the center of the city.

the many insects in this area are two of the reasons it is almost without people and of little economic value. But, as one visitor reports below, the Amazon is not all jungle and bugs.

Our plane puts down on the south shore of the Amazon at Belém [Brazil]. This hot, bustling port . . . is the gateway to the big river. Naked scaffolds of new buildings push up through the mango trees lining the main avenue, crowding out the tiled houses that have been there since colonial days. . . .

Noisy merchants shout directions as they unload rubber, lumber, jaguar skins, alligator hides, and even live wild animals from upriver. The waiting cargo boats patiently ride the waves. . . .

We board one of the smaller, wood-burning steamers that carries supplies to the trading posts along the river. It takes two or three weeks in this craft to chug along 1,000 miles of the muddy waters of the lower Amazon to Manaus.

As we slide past forest-clad banks, the river broadens until at times we lose sight of the opposite shore. Now and then we pass a palm-thatched mud hut with its own tiny wharf and dugout canoe. . . .

As we draw into Manaus some of the lighter craft in the river traffic all about us hitch rides with our steamer. . . . We cast off our lines at Manaus' floating dock, built on pontoons to rise with the water level when the river is in flood. . . . On the docks brown-skinned stevedores, their backs piled high with wares ranging from bananas to pots and pans, scurry antlike in and out of the surrounding bedlam.

Manaus and its 200,000 people look so scrubbed and starched that it is hard to believe that we are in the tropics. They go briskly about their business among tile-fronted buildings. . . . Dominating the hilly city . . . is the ornate gold-domed opera house which once brought Italian opera to the jungle. After a long decline, Manaus once more prospers as a result of new industry: an oil refinery, a jute mill, plywood factories, a bottling plant, among others.

Ibid., pp. 44–46.

Large desert areas are found all over Latin America. Conditions in these areas make it almost impossible to raise crops in an area which already has a hard time feeding its people.

In direct contrast to the river and jungle areas are those which suffer from not enough rain. Among these are the "dry" areas of northwestern Mexico, northeastern Brazil, and the southern and northwestern parts of Argentina. The driest part of Latin America is the Atacama Desert. It runs along the northern coast of Chile and Peru for almost two thousand miles. Almost no vegetation grows on the Atacama. In fact, some settlements on this desert have never recorded rainfall. The coastal desert population is scattered about in mining camps and cities which serve the mining industry. These cities, which are surrounded by dry, barren country, must import almost everything, including food, fuel, and water.

What is so unique about the Amazon? Why do you think there are so many different life styles along the river? What, if anything, do you think could be done to make the Amazon river basin more populated and productive?

A Hard Life—The *Altiplano* . . . The *altiplano* is the high plain of Peru and Bolivia. It is one of the poorest areas in the world. Most of the people who live there are Indians who, even though they work hard, lead a life of poverty. As noted in the newspaper report below, the *altiplano* and its people pose a serious problem for Bolivia.

A quarter of a century after the revolution which was to free them from serfdom, Bolivia's 3 million Indians still live short, hard lives on a deserted plateau two miles above the sea.

Indians make up more than two-thirds of the population of Bolivia today.

Even with their numbers, these descendants of the Inca and Aymara people live almost entirely outside the country's economic system. They do not earn or spend money but merely scratch out a bare living on the bleak altiplano.

Recent estimates put life expectancy nationally at 49, with the figure for the Indians of the altiplano nearer 30.

There are almost no medical facilities in rural areas and infant deaths stand at 150 deaths per 1,000 births, one of the highest figures in the world.

A recent unofficial survey shows that the average Bolivian eats only six grams of meat a year, which means that the peasants are too poor to eat any meat at all.

One of the main barriers to Bolivian development is Bolivia itself. The country is divided into four different areas—the high, narrow altiplano with tropical valleys to the east of it, then a vast, rich but underpopulated plain and finally thick jungle toward the border with Brazil.

Almost three-quarters of the people live on the altiplano, the 10% of the country which has the major cities and the important mineral deposits—but also the poorest land for farming.

The altiplano is at an average 14,000 feet. The earth is poor and the climate hard. The air is so thin that the Indians who live there have extra red corpuscles in their blood to make up for the lack of oxygen.

Early plans to move highlanders in the richer plains to the east failed because they could not get used to the climate or fell ill from the tropical diseases.

The East, which could be very rich, is almost empty, and more humane plans than before are now going on to help highlanders move to the tropical plains.

Socially the Indians have come a long way since the times when they were advertised as part of the goods and property of estates put up for sale, but they have yet to find a place in the country's economic life.

Until they do, these people will go on living in poverty.

Adapted from Harvey Morris of Reuters, "Life of Bolivian Indians Remains Harsh," which appeared in the *Los Angeles Times*, March 31, 1977, Part 1–A, pp. 1–2.

How does the physical environment of the area affect the Bolivian Indians? The economy and development of Bolivia?

Why would one of the main barriers to Bolivian development be Bolivia itself?

How, if at all, can the problems of the *altiplano* and the Indians living there be solved?

EXPLORATION

The maps below show some important features of Latin America. After studying them, answer the following questions.

What are the principal geographic features of Latin America? What areas of Latin America have mountains? Plains? Jungles? Deserts? Which areas of Latin America have the warmest weather? The coolest? The most moderate temperatures? In which of these climates would it be the most pleasant to live? How does altitude affect the temperature?

Which areas get the most rain? The least? How does the amount of rain influence the geography of an area? How does it affect human habitation in an area?

In what areas is the Latin American population most heavily concentrated? What are the geographical features of those areas? Why do you think the people have settled in these particular areas?

Based on the information given in this chapter and in the maps, explain the relationship between the environment, the population density, and the life styles of Latin America.

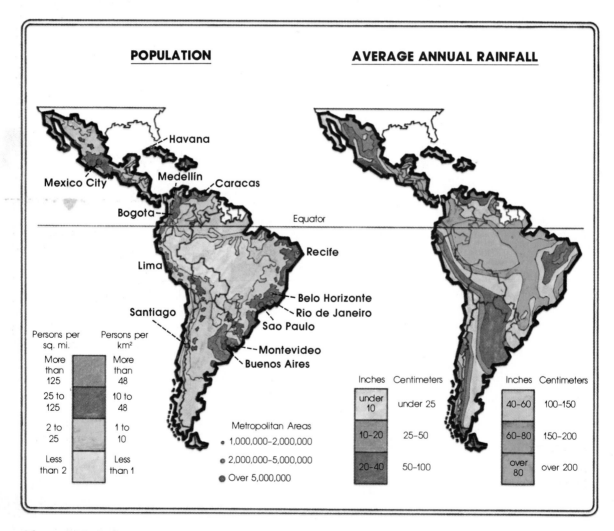

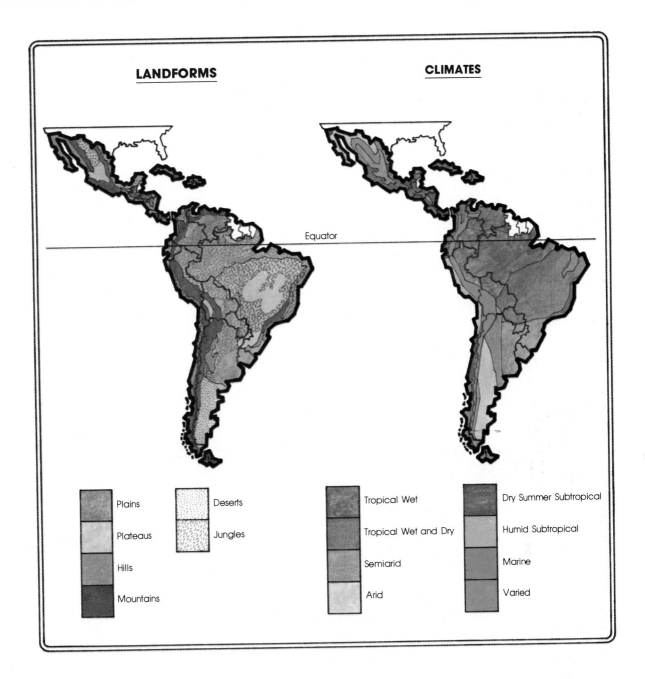

LANDFORMS

CLIMATES

Equator

Plains
Plateaus
Hills
Mountains

Deserts
Jungles

Tropical Wet
Tropical Wet and Dry
Semiarid
Arid

Dry Summer Subtropical
Humid Subtropical
Marine
Varied

Review

varied environment
Andes
pampas
llanos

gaucho
river systems
Amazon

Manaus
Atacama Desert
altiplano

2

In what way is Latin America a "melting pot"?

What contributions have the various peoples made to the development of Latin America?

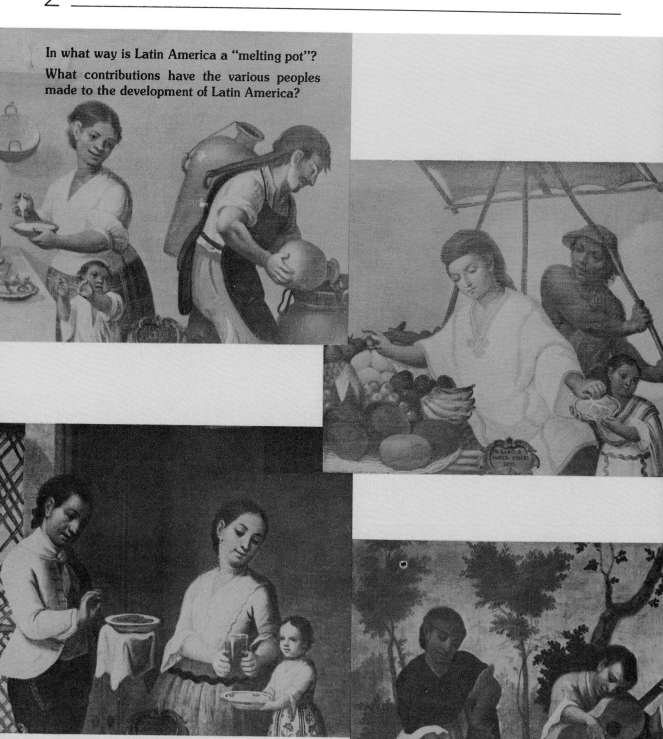

The Human Diversity

. . . there are cities where the African darkens the streets, and cities to which the Indian gives his copper hue, and cities whiter than Berlin. To further [accent] these contrasts, there is the mestizo, the man whose blood is half white and half Indian; the mulatto, who is half black and half white; the zambo, who is half [black] and half Indian. . . .

For four hundred years men from the four corners of the earth . . . have been mixing with the [Indians] of these lands. It is the most amazing experiment in the intermingling of bloods that history has ever witnessed. . . . So many circumstances have influenced the color scheme that today the racial map is like Joseph's coat. . . .

Nor should one have illusions about the language. There has been a great division from the start, for ours is a dual world, one part of which speaks Portuguese—Brazil—and the other . . . Spanish—Spanish America. But inland, in the heart of the continent, other accents are heard.

There are 300 million people in Latin America—Europeans, Indians, Asians, blacks, and many different mixtures of these groups. Due to intermarriage, over one half of the people are of mixed blood. Mestizos form the largest single group. Then, there are about 20 million mulattos. Each country is different. In Argentina, there are few blacks, but across the border in Brazil, there are many. In Bolivia the Indian and the mestizo are the largest groups, while in Peru half of the people are white or mestizo. In Mexico, the whites are in the minority.

The same is true of the language of Latin America. Most people think it is Spanish. But the people of Brazil speak Portuguese. And each nation has its own dialects and Indian tongues. In Paraguay there is Guaraní; in Peru, Quechua; and in Bolivia, Aymara. Because of this, Latin America truly can be called the "melting pot" of the Western Hemisphere.

Germán Arciniegas, *The Green Continent*, trans. Harriet De Onís (New York: Alfred A. Knopf, Inc., 1944), pp. xiv, xviii–xix.

The first Americans were the Indians. They are thought to have come to the Western Hemisphere across the Bering Strait thousands of years ago. By the time Columbus arrived in the New World, Indians called Aztecs, Mayas, and Incas already had their own great civilizations. In 1520 the Spanish conqueror Hernando Cortés described the city of Tenochtitlán to King Charles I of Spain. When Cortés wrote his description, Tenochtitlán was the Aztec capital of Mexico. Today the modern capital Mexico City sits on the same site.

The great city of Tenochtitlán is built in the midst of this salt lake, and it is two leagues [about six miles] from the heart of the city to any point on the mainland. Four causeways lead to it, all made by hand and some twelve feet wide. . . . The principal streets are very broad and straight, the majority of them being of beaten earth, but a few and at least half the smaller thoroughfares are waterways along which they pass in their canoes. Moreover, even the principal streets have openings at regular distances so that the water can freely pass from one to another, and these openings . . . are spanned by great bridges of huge beams, very stoutly put together, so firm indeed that over many of them ten horsemen can ride at once. . . .

The city has many open squares in which markets are continuously held and the general business of buying and selling proceeds. One square . . . is . . . completely surrounded by arcades where there are daily more than sixty thousand folk buying and selling. Every kind of merchandise such as may be met with in every land is for sale there. . . .

The city of Tenochtitlán was the capital of the Aztec empire. It was the symbol of the empire's wealth and power. This is the ancient Great Temple.

The American Museum of Natural History

There are a very large number of mosques [temples] or dwelling places for their idols . . . in the chief of which their priests live continuously, so that in addition to the actual temples containing idols there are sumptuous lodgings. . . . Among these temples there is one chief one . . . whose size and magnificence no human tongue could describe. For it is so big that within the lofty wall which entirely circles it one could set a town of fifteen thousand inhabitants. . . .

There are three large halls in the great mosque where the principal idols are to be found, all of immense size and height and richly decorated with sculptured figures both in wood and stone, and within these halls are other smaller temples branching off from them and entered by doors so small that no daylight ever reaches them. . . .

The city contains many large and fine houses. . . . All possess in addition to large and elegant apartments very delightful flower gardens of every kind, both on the ground level and on the upper storeys.

Along one of the causeways connecting this great city with the mainland two pipes are constructed of masonry, each two paces broad and about as high as a man, one of which conveys a stream of water very clear and fresh and about the thickness of a man's body right to the centre of the city, which all can use for drinking and other purposes. The other pipe which is empty is used when it is desired to clean the former. . . . The water is sold from canoes in all the streets, the manner of their taking it from the pipes being in this wise: the canoes place themselves under the bridges where the troughs are to be found, and from above the canoes are filled [with water] by men who are especially paid for this work.

There are many cultural treasures in Mexico. Far right: This Mayan calendar stone shows 584 days. The Mayan civilization reached its peak between 400 and 900 A.D. Right: This Mayan clay container came from Palengue, in the Yucatán Peninsula.

Museo Nacional de Historia

Rich Brommer

The European conquerors destroyed much of what the Indians had built. Yet they needed—and used—the Indians. They relied on their skilled labor to do the building. Many Indian words became part of the Spanish and Portuguese languages. Still more important, the Spaniards and the Portuguese married Indians. This resulted in a new ethnic group—the mestizo.

Today the Indian may be a farmer high in the Andes or a hunter in the jungles of the Amazon. Wherever they still survive in large numbers, the Indians have tried to preserve their own culture. In Bolivia, Ecuador, Guatemala, Mexico, and Peru, they have kept their own dress, language, and social structure. Often the Indians prefer to keep apart from the rest of the nation. They use their own ways of farming. They produce just enough to stay alive. Living in small villages, they divide their work among their people according to tradition. They may use tools like the ones their ancestors used. Even when their religion and dress show a Western influence, the Indians try to keep enough of their own culture to make them a little different from the rest of the country. As noted below, however, the one area in which most Indians have not become more Western is in the language they speak.

> . . . it's all Spanish, more or less, and one can make himself understood . . . more or less. Until he enters one of the many zones where Spanish still has not supplanted the Indian language. And these zones are many, vast, and, despite years of effort by governments, missionaries, and others, seemingly unchangeable. For example, in Mexico today there are still over a million Indians who have not learned Spanish; most speak Náhuatl, the Aztec tongue. In Bolivia, the majority speak Aymara or the Inca language, Quechua . . . ; in Chile, a third of a million people speak Araucana (but most of these also speak Spanish); in Paraguay, Guaraní is spoken outside of the capital, but again, most of the people also speak Spanish; in Guatemala, over half the population speak Quiche rather than Spanish.

What does Cortés' letter about Tenochtitlán suggest about the level of Indian civilization? What do you think Cortés thought about Tenochtitlán?

How does today's Indian culture compare with the one described by Cortés?

In your opinion, why have the local Indian languages not been replaced by Spanish in various regions of Latin America?

From *El Gringo: The Yankee Image in Latin America*, pp. 15–16, by D. H. Radler. Copyright, 1962, by the author. Reprinted with permission of the publisher, Chilton Book Company, Radnor, PA.

People from Europe and Asia influenced the growth of Latin America in many ways. Above left: This European has lived in Buenos Aires for many years. Above right: European styles have had an effect on architecture.

The Europeans . . . The settlers who came from Europe did much to shape the vast area south of the Rio Grande. The Portuguese in Brazil and the Spaniards in the other regions tried to pattern the life in their new land after the one they had known in Europe. They introduced new kinds of grains and fruits as well as horses and other domesticated animals. They also brought with them many kinds of technology. And, because they had the money and the knowledge, they took advantage of the mineral wealth of their new land.

Until the early 1800's, when the Latin American colonies won their independence, about two thousand Spanish and Portuguese immigrants came to Latin America each year. After that, more Europeans than ever landed on Latin American shores. From the middle of the nineteenth century until World War I, 12 million flocked to Latin America. Most of these people were from Spain and Portugal. But, this time, there were a great many Italians, English, and Germans, too. Most of these people settled in Argentina, Uruguay, and the extreme southern part of Brazil. Today those people and their descendants make up a large part of the peoples of Argentina and Uruguay. For this reason, those countries are known as "immigrant nations." The European immigrants brought more than their skills. They also brought a willingness to work hard. As a result, they have been largely responsible for the economic progress of the areas in which they settled.

What did the European immigrants contribute to Latin America?

Blacks in Latin America quickly adopted the customs, language, and culture of their new homeland. This is a May Day celebration in Cuba.

Fred Ward for Black Star

The Blacks . . . In the 1500's, the European settlers began to bring black slaves from Africa to work in the tropical areas of Brazil. This slave trade was ended in the 1800's. But during the three hundred years of the slave trade, at least 15 million Africans were brought by force into the Western Hemisphere. Of this total, Brazil alone received some 12 million slaves.

Both as slaves and as free people, blacks played an important role in the development of Latin America. One author explains:

> . . . the [black] became the . . . means for the colonization of vast American regions. Cotton and tobacco in the United States, sugar in the West Indies, cocoa in Venezuela, sugar, mining, and coffee in Brazil, and a thousand other kinds of enterprise everywhere else were dependent upon the [black]. In Brazil the [black] was so much the laborer that no one else seemed to labor at all. . . . the [black] seemed to be the most intelligent person . . . because every occupation, skilled and unskilled, was in the [blacks'] hands. Even in Buenos Aires theirs was the hand that built the best churches. They were the fieldhands, and in many places the miners; they were the cooks, the laundresses, . . . the nurses about the houses, the coachmen, and the laborers on the wharves. But they were also the skilled artisans who built the houses, carved the saints in the churches, constructed the carriages, forged the beautiful ironwork . . . and played in the orchestras. The [black], slave and free, was the living hand that [decorated] the setting and provided the art and the spice for the cultured, easy, and carefree life that some of the New World plantation centers [delighted] in for so long a time.

Frank Tannenbaum, *Slave and Citizen: The Negro in the Americas* (New York: Alfred A. Knopf, Inc., 1946), pp. 39–40.

The hand labor of the black people produced much of the farming wealth of parts of Brazil and the islands of the Caribbean. Today there are about 25 million blacks in Latin America. Some are in trade and commerce. Some own their own businesses. Still others are artists and musicians. Yet, despite their rich heritage, the opportunities open to many blacks are still limited.

Why did so many blacks settle in Latin America?

In what ways did the Europeans depend on blacks?

Explain this statement: "Without the blacks the texture of American life would have been different." Do you agree with the statement? Why or why not?

Asians . . . A new dimension has been added to the ethnic composition in recent years as groups of Asians have come to live in Latin America. One group, the Chinese, have made their homes in Peru, Cuba, and Panama. They first were brought into these countries as laborers. Today most are merchants, and Chinese shops and restaurants are found in many cities.

In addition, there are 200,000 Japanese who have settled in Brazil. They came at the start to work on the coffee plantations. It was the Japanese who introduced jute to Brazil. Today jute is used in the bags which hold Brazil's coffee. The jute industry provides a cash crop for farmers who once lived off what Brazil nuts and rubber they could find. Today the Japanese are engaged in farming, fishing, trade and commerce, and manufacturing. Lately some of these settlers have begun to leave Brazil. They are going to Peru to see if they can establish successful settlements there.

In what ways are Asian settlers contributing to Latin America?

Steven A. Seidman

A small number of people from Asia have come to Latin America. This boy is one of these people.

A New Way of Life . . .
Many of the Maya Indians of Mexico have changed their way of life in recent years. Progress has caught up with them. An American couple who lived in Mexico for many years describe their experiences with this new breed of Maya.

When we lived at Cobá [a village in Yucatán] we returned to Mérida [a city in Yucatán] frequently and visited with friends. Tránsita and her aunt, Modesta [two Mayas], gave Ann and me embroidery lessons. They showed us how to draw threads from white cloth for openwork, and make half-forgotten designs in vivid thread. We spent several afternoons with them, gossiping and joking and trying to master the complex work that seemed so easy for them.

"Girls today don't want to do hand embroidery," complained Tránsita. "They wear huipils [dresses] made by machine. When I was young, girls stayed home, but now they want to go all the time. Always in the streets, going somewhere.

"We had a big fiesta every year . . . and every year we girls made a new huipil for it. The day after the fiesta we would start making a new one. It took that long.

"My papa would buy the cloth and the colors of thread we wanted, and then he would say, 'Now I've done my part. The rest is up to you.'

"Many nights my sisters and I got up at two in the morning and sat around a little table with one candle, whispering and giggling and embroidering until dawn."

She laughed and shook her head. "Now always in the streets. Everything by machine."

Tránsita's friend Maria Ybarra came to live with us in Mérida when she was a girl of 15. She had grown up on the hacienda Lepán. . . . Her mother is Maya; her father was a Korean sent to Yucatán as a child laborer before the turn of the century, and given a Spanish name.

Maria learned Catholicism in the hacienda chapel, Maya rituals and stories from her mother and elderly godparents who lived on a ranch nearby. Maya was her first language, and the Spanish that she knew she taught me—with a Maya accent.

Now she is a Mérida matron, married to a skilled stonemason, and the mother of five. Her Spanish is perfect. She speaks Maya occasionally but her husband . . . and the children do not speak it at all. The family has converted to the Mormon faith. They are an urban family—part of Mexico's expanding middle class.

On our latest visit to Mérida, we spent several evenings with them, enjoying the cool patio while the children watched television inside. The family motorcycle was parked nearby. . . .

They told us of trips to Mexico City. Maria and some of the children planned a visit to the new beach resort of Cancún in Quintana Roo [a new state in Mexico].

She spent an afternoon retelling me old tales, ceremonies and cures that she had learned as a child from her relatives and godparents. But that young girl who embroidered huipils and made a hetzmek ceremony for our son so many years ago was now living in another world.

From the Special Publication, *The Mysterious Maya*. © National Geographic Society, 1977, pp. 191–192.

Compare and contrast the attitudes of Tránsita and Maria. Which do you think is the more common one? Explain. Do you think that age had anything to do with their attitudes? Explain.

What do the comments suggest about the future of some Indians in Mexico? In other parts of Latin America?

EXPLORATION

Each of the pictures illustrates a different ethnic group in Latin America. Which of the people might have had ancestors who came from Asia? From Africa? From Europe? Which might be able to trace their ancestry to more than one area of the world? How do these people illustrate the theory of Latin America as the "melting pot" of the Western Hemisphere?

Based on the information in the chapter, explain how each ethnic group has contributed to the Latin American way of life.

Rich Brommer

Courtesy Inter-American Development Bank by David Mangurian

Alpha Photo

Standard Oil of New Jersey Collection, University of Louisville Photographic Archives

David Mangurian

Steven A. Seidman

Review

mestizo
mulatto
Tenochtitlán

Indian cultures
European influence

black influence
Asian influence

3

How important are social class distinctions in Latin America?

How does social class affect the Latin American family?

At the Root of Living

Perico G—is 22 years old. He is a mestizo, with more white than Indian blood. He is medium sized, wiry, and agile. . . . He grew up near Valencia [Venezuela], where his father was a share-cropper. His father died when Perico was twelve, and he had to leave school to go to work. . . . When Perico was sixteen he joined the Venezuelan navy, where he served for three years in the engine room of a destroyer. After his discharge he was unemployed for almost a year. . . . finally he and a friend hitchhiked to Maracaibo, where Perico found work as a helper on a tank farm. . . . His mother and two brothers joined him about a year ago, and the family moved into a government-sponsored housing development where they have a four-room house made of concrete block, for which they pay a very low rent. Perico's mother is delighted with the house, which has window screens and is relatively free of insects. Perico is a union member. . . . He . . . gets a paid vacation, free medical care, and the privilege of taking training courses at company expense.

Perico belongs to a soccer club, which takes up a good deal of his spare time. He met a girl at one of the soccer club parties and is seriously interested in her. Marriage presents difficulties, however, as Perico is the principal breadwinner for his family, and his girl does not want to share a four-room house with Perico, his mother, and two brothers. Perico does not know what to do about this.

Perico is typical of the many Latin Americans who are forming a new middle class. He has a chance to move upward in social class, in his job, and in his style of life. As Perico's life changes, so will that of his family. Traditionally, the family is the basic social unit in Latin America. Also traditionally, how the family lives depends on its social class. Even today, the "rules" are different for the members of each of the three social classes of Latin America.

Raymond E. Crist and Edward P. Leahy, *Venezuela: Search for a Middle Ground* (New York: Van Nostrand Reinhold Company, 1969), pp. 53–54.

In some places, such as the United States, the word "family" most often means the nuclear group of mother, father, and children. But in Latin America it has a slightly different meaning. "Family" also includes grandparents and great-grandparents, uncles and aunts, nieces and nephews, distant cousins, and godparents. Godparents are people chosen by the mother and father to sponsor their new baby. They are concerned with the religious and moral training of their godchild. They also take care of the child if something should happen to the parents.

For the most part, the Latin American family is large. It also is closely knit. Family members try to live near each other. When they cannot do so, they still try to keep in constant contact with each other. The family is the center for most social activities. Birthdays, weddings, and the like are celebrated by a gathering of the entire family. The family also acts as a mutual-aid society. This means that family members are expected to help a relative in distress or to share with the others any good fortune they may have.

But times are changing. Among the rich and the lower class, the family is still very powerful. The rich want to protect their wealth and prestige. The poor want to help fight off economic disaster when it comes. But among the people of the urban middle class, it is different. In the past, most young people remained in their parents' homes even after they married. Today, many move away. This makes contact between relatives more difficult. Those who do not know how to read or write or are too poor to use the telephone regularly find it especially hard to keep in touch.

Another reason for the family's loss of influence is the attitude of business and government. At one time a person's family ties helped a lot when it came to getting a job. Today ability is more important as a basis for hiring. Then, too, the family used to take care of the welfare and education of its members. Today these are the responsibility of the state.

In what ways does the Latin American concept of family differ from yours? How is it the same?

What are the benefits of the Latin American view of family? What are the drawbacks?

Why is the influence of the traditional family beginning to lessen?

Hard Work, Little Reward . . . There are three social classes in most Latin American nations—the upper class, the middle class, and the lower class. The largest social class by far in most of these nations is the lower class. Within the rural lower class, the biggest group is composed of peasants. Some of the peasants own and work their own small plots of land.

Some work part-time on *haciendas*, large estates owned by the wealthy. Others work only for the *hacienda*, tilling the fields in return for a small plot of land which must support their families. Often the peasants work the same land that their fathers and grandfathers did during colonial times. The second group of the rural lower class is made up of the wage-hands. They generally work on the large, modern commercial farms that raise export crops such as sugar cane, cotton, coffee, and bananas. Their wages are low, and their work often is seasonal.

Although there are still more poor people in the country than in the city, the number of urban poor is on the increase. This is due to the millions of people who have migrated from the country to the cities in recent years. But jobs in the urban areas are scarce, and often the newcomers have no skills. Many of them cannot read or write. They can find only poor-paying, unskilled jobs as factory workers, construction hands, street vendors, bootblacks, or domestics. As a result, it is not often that these migrants can escape poverty.

The poorest, however, are those who have no source of regular work. They think themselves fortunate if they can find work as laborers on construction projects or as carriers of firewood or water. If they fail to find even this type of work, they may become beggars. Socially, they often are rejected even by the other groups within the lower class.

The poverty of the people of the lower class has a strong influence on their way of life. For example, most marriages are common-law unions, unofficial marriages without legal or religious ceremony. These marriages are accepted for several reasons. The cost of a formal wedding and the celebration that follows it could force a bride's family into debt for many

Rich Brommer

In Latin America, jobs can be hard to find. Many people have to earn a living as best they can. Here is a produce market in Xochimilco, Mexico.

years. Then, too, there is the problem of divorce. There are no legal or religious problems if such a marriage does not work out. The couple just breaks up.

Family life under such conditions of poverty is hard. Because there is so little money, young children are expected to go to work. In the country, a very young boy will be given errands to run. Before he reaches his teens, he probably will be working in the fields. In the city, a boy is expected to have a part-time or a full-time job by the time he is eight years old. Girls must begin at a very early age to do household chores and take care of the younger children. There is little time for school and a formal education.

In most cases, there is an accepted code of family life, such as the one described below:

> Villagers in this small Mexican village agree about ideal role behavior within the family: the husband is dominant. The wife should be faithful and humble, careful in managing family resources, and kind and loving with her children. Children are expected to show affection and mutual and economic support.
>
> Almost all men turn what they earn over to their wives, expecting to be given money for expenses when they ask for it. Cash is kept in a locked chest or put in a pot hidden behind the woodpile or placed on a beam where it looks like one among dozens of old vessels and molds. Care is taken to make sure that no one outside the family knows where money is kept. In addition to these working funds, many women try to keep an *alcancía*, a piggy bank, in which spare coins are dropped from time to time, to be kept for an emergency.
>
> Some husbands, however, insist on keeping all money themselves, handing out daily expense money to their wives in small quantities. This is often a source of irritation. These are the really dominant husbands. These husbands hold a tight rein on their wives and children, and do not allow them to mix carelessly with other people. The wife of such a man is expected to talk with other women only to make purchases and to have nixtamal [limed corn kernels] ground at the mill. Daughters are closely watched, sent to Mass, but not allowed to stay around afterward, or to stroll the streets or visit friends. Life with such men is not easy, but women feel that a wife must accept her husband as he is and that she must put up with what fate has brought her.

Who makes up the lower class in Latin America?
In a lower class family, what is the role of the male? Of the female?
How, if at all, does lack of money affect family life?

Adapted from George M. Foster, *Tzintzuntzan: Mexican Peasants in a Changing World,* pp. 57–60. Copyright © 1967 by Little, Brown and Company (Inc.). Reprinted by permission.

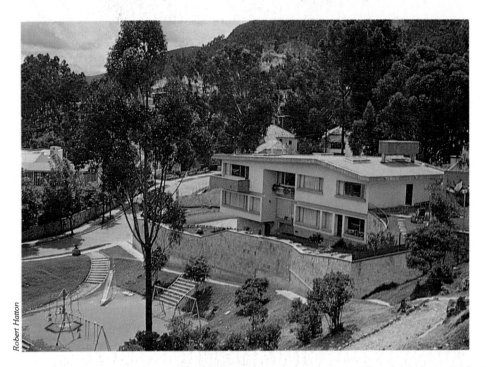

Robert Hatton

There is little contact between the social classes in Latin America. This home in Bogotá, Colombia, contrasts with the living conditions of most of the city's residents.

An Easier Life . . . Latin America's upper class is made up of two distinct groups. One is the aristocracy, made up, for the most part, of descendants of the wealthy and titled landowners of the past. In some ways, today's aristocrats lead very much the same kind of life that their ancestors did in the 1800's. They are, in most cases, well-educated and cultured. They do no manual labor. The men manage their landholdings while the women direct the house servants. Most of the year they live in the city. In the past, this group based its wealth and prestige on old family names and the ownership of large rural landholdings. This is still true to some extent. But in recent years, fewer and fewer aristocrats depend on land alone for their wealth. Today many are engaged in business.

The other group is the "nouveaux riches," the new rich, who have made their fortunes in this century. Most were not born wealthy but have become rich through their own efforts and hard work. Because the "nouveaux riches" usually lack aristocratic background and culture, some aristocrats look down on them. Still, the two groups have much in common, especially in their family life. In both groups, the male expects to make all the decisions. All who live under his roof, be they relatives or servants, are expected to obey him and to go along with what he decides. Women were, and in most cases still are, supposed to spend their time running the household and raising children. Education is important. Children are expected to graduate from high school and from college.

The Castros, described below, live in Lomas de Chapultepec, a nice residential section of Mexico City. This family and the life it leads is typical of the upper class "nouveaux riches."

> David Castro . . . owned a cement business . . . two stores and two apartment houses, a cottage in Acapulco, and his home in Lomas. . . . Their home was . . . located in . . . Lomas. A high iron gate, kept locked day and night, enclosed the driveway and the ill-kept garden of English grass and flowering plants. The two-story white stone and cement house had a living room, dining room, kitchen, and bath downstairs, and three bedrooms and bath upstairs. . . .
>
> The family kept three servants, a cook, a chambermaid, and a laundress, all of whom lived in servants' quarters on the roof. . . .
>
> On the roof of the house Eufemia, the laundress, was washing the large pile of clothes which the Castro family soiled every day. When Eufemia had first come to work in this house she had been surprised at the quantity of clothing the family owned and by the fact that they changed their clothes every day. And the big cement sink on the roof, with its running water and built-in washboard, was impressive. . . .
>
> At eleven a bell rang twice in the kitchen, a signal that the Señores were awake and getting ready to come down for breakfast. Usually on holidays they got up a little earlier, at ten or ten-thirty, but David had come home late the night before, . . . and Isabel had a cold and was quite willing to stay on in bed. On school days Isabel had to rise at six-thirty to get the children under way for the day. They attended three different private schools, and the three schedules for breakfast, lunch, and the school bus in addition to her husband's independent routine, quite filled Isabel's mornings and afternoons. . . .
>
> At twelve o'clock the family sat down at the table. Isabel rang a little silver bell, and Josefina, who waited on the table, came in with a platter of pancakes.
>
> "Mamá," said Lourdes, "just give me one."
>
> "You'll eat as many as your mother gives you, baby," her father said. "I don't know why you all fuss so much about eating. It would be a good thing if you knew what it is to be really hungry."
>
> "I bet you don't know, papá," Manuel said.
>
> "Why shouldn't I know? Do you think I've always had money? I've pulled myself up to where I am today but it's meant plenty of hard work. But I always took home money to my mother no matter what. And I never answered her back the way you all do to your mother. Now shut up and eat, fast and well. . . ."

From *Five Families: Mexican Case Studies in the Culture of Poverty* by Oscar Lewis, pp. 296, 297, 298, 305. © 1959 by Basic Books, Inc., Publishers, New York.

What groups make up the upper class of Latin America?

In upper class families, what is the role of the male? The female?

How do their family roles compare and contrast with those of the lower class?

What are the differences in attitude toward children between upper and lower class parents? Which of these differences, if any, do you think are a result of social class?

John Pennington/The Picture Cube

The modern architecture and two-car garage of this home in Honduras show some of the benefits of economic development.

A New Generation . . . The Latin American middle class is largely a product of the twentieth century. Industry has grown, and there are more white-collar jobs. Government needs more civil servants, teachers, and different kinds of experts. There are more educational opportunities. This has made it possible for more people to prepare for careers in medicine, law, and journalism. At times, it is hard to say just who is a member of the middle class. Incomes range from those of well-to-do bankers to those of poorly paid civil servants or clerks. Housing ranges from high-priced homes in some parts of town to lower-cost ones in other areas.

A family in Quito, Ecuador, proudly stands in front of their modern home in the northern section of the city.

David Mangurian

In most middle class households, just as in those of the other classes, the husband or father expects to make all the important decisions. As a result, until recently, most middle class women led very sheltered lives. They seldom left the house. Today, however, many middle class wives and daughters work outside the home in an effort to increase the family income.

The members of the Pilomia family of Brazil are typical of those in an upper middle class family. Their way of life is described below.

Seventeen-year-old Túlia Pilomia went back to Brazil following her year of study at McLean High School in Virginia. It had been fun to learn about different customs by living with a family in the United States. . . . But she was delighted to rejoin her own family in the town of Goiânia on the central plateau.

The Pilomia household consists of Túlia's father, who is both a medical doctor and a tax official as well as farm owner, her mother, their three daughters, two sons, and three servants. Telma, one of Túlia's sisters, is only a year younger. Their sister Tércia is fourteen and in junior high—or *ginásio*, as this middle school is called in Brazil.

Of the two boys in the family, only eleven-year-old Francisco, Jr., is Túlia's real brother. Julival, now twelve, was "adopted" by the family. . . .

Túlia's swarthy father is from Natal, at the tip of the Brazilian "bulge." His father died when he was a lad. To help support the family he made and sold wooden spoons. Determined to study medicine, he worked his way through the University of Bahia. . . .

During the mornings Dr. Pilomia sees his patients. Many are too poor to pay but have been coming to see him for years and he refuses to turn away old friends. After lunch he becomes an official tax collector. . . . He also owns some truck farms, run by tenant farmers who also raise a few cattle. Although the farms help him pay his bills, they are something of a hobby with him too. On weekends he piles his family into his Brazilian-made Microbus to make the rounds. The servants also go along. . . .

Reprinted by permission of the Publisher, Thomas Nelson, Inc. From the book *Brazil, Awakening Giant*, pp. 61–64. Copyright © 1967 by Kathleen Seegers.

Mrs. Pilomia keeps endlessly busy. She has a farm of her own—a small one called a *chácara*—which raises food for the family table. She often drives out there. . . . She also raises money for [a] school [for the poor] and works for various other charities. Besides running the household, she putters in the flower garden, [and] helps the children with their lessons. . . .

Tércia . . . goes to a public coeducational school. Up at 6:30 A.M., she gulps down a glass of orange juice. . . . If she's not feeling fat, though, she has an egg. Some mornings she drinks cocoa, others coffee mixed with warm milk. Then she has to run, for she's due at school at 7:30. She is studying Portuguese, math, history, geography, biology, English, and design. She attends school only in the mornings, with a fifteen-minute recess at 9:30.

After lunch she takes a music lesson or goes to speech class. . . . A sports-lover, she plays basketball and volleyball. With her teenage friends she takes time out for an afternoon snack—usually bread-and-butter and a bottle of *guaraná* [a carbonated soft drink sold only in Brazil].

After dinner the family frequently watches TV. Many programs, such as Telma's favorite "Bonanza," are imported from the States. Her father likes to watch the fights; her mother enjoys the cartoons.

Nearly every year Mrs. Pilomia takes the children to the beach at Santos for a two-week vacation by the sea. In Goiânia the girls swim in a pool on Sunday mornings after church. Sunday afternoons they seldom miss the six o'clock movie. Afterward, they stroll home arm-in-arm past the local boys, who collect along the main street to flirt.

Why did the Latin American middle class begin to grow in the twentieth century?

In what ways is the middle class family similar to the lower class family? To the upper class family? How does it differ from a lower class family? From an upper class family?

In your opinion, does the family life of the Latin American middle class compare with that of a middle class family in your country? In what ways are they alike? In what ways are they different?

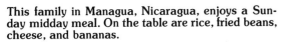

This family in Managua, Nicaragua, enjoys a Sunday midday meal. On the table are rice, fried beans, cheese, and bananas.

Changing Roles . . . In Latin America, the docile position of women was a carry-over from the past. Until recent years, men ordered, and women obeyed. But the role of the Latin American woman is changing. The account which follows talks about the why and how of that change.

In the Guaraní language, widely spoken in central South America, the word for wife means "the person who serves me."

This concept of woman as an object, to be cherished and protected but also for most purposes, the property of her father or husband, is a trait still almost universal in Latin America today. It is less apparent in modern capitals than in the provinces. But to some degree it influences the life of nearly every woman.

Until 25 years ago, this passive role was in the laws of most of Latin America. Women's rights were restricted or did not exist, and married women were so enslaved by their husbands legally that men, in effect, "owned" their wives.

Since then, under pressure from groups supporting women's rights, most of the laws have been erased. Women can now vote and hold public office in all 20 Latin American nations.

However, on the books of every country except Uruguay are one or more laws which discriminate against married women in some ways or make them less equal than their husbands.

Although some legal obstacles remain, more progress toward equality for women has been made since the end of World War II than in all of the hemisphere's history. The rule of equal pay for equal work exists in the laws of every country, although they are not always obeyed.

Determined women have gained success in the professions in nearly every Latin American country. In politics, women are making their presence and their opinions felt. Women judges, national legislators and mayors are no longer rarities. Women are flocking to colleges in search of career training.

A working wife has always been a reflection on the maleness of a Latin American middle class male. That taboo is melting as more married women go to work to give the family such luxuries as a car. Slow to catch up with changes in laws, tradition dictates that most women are passed from the domination of their fathers to that of their husbands. A woman from a traditional home, in the words of a Brazilian newspaper reporter "is free to marry any man she chooses as long as he's the one of her father's choice." Unmarried women in such families are expected to live at home and obey all paternal rules even though they may be in their 30's and 40's and have successful careers.

Many women, especially in rural areas, do not even understand that there should be a change. Many more, aware that women have new status, make no effort to exercise their rights. Others object to the changes, siding with the male view that restrictions exist for their protection.

Adapted from David F. Belnap, "Some Gains, Sí But You've Still Got Long, Long Way to Go, Señorita!" *Los Angeles Times*, August 18, 1969, p. 17. Copyright, 1969, Los Angeles Times. Reprinted by permission.

In what ways is the role of women changing in Latin America? Why do you think it has taken so long for Latin American women to gain any sort of equality? What are some of the factors which have held back female equality in Latin American nations? What are some of the factors which have contributed to any gains made by the women?

In your opinion, how does the role of the Latin American woman compare with that of the North American woman?

EXPLORATION

There are many well-known Latin American sayings. These three are Brazilian:

"A son's first duty is to his father."

"He who at birth is worth two cents can never be worth much more."

"When you are poor, even your footsteps are gloomy."

What does each of these sayings mean to you?

What does each suggest about the Latin American attitude toward family or social class?

David Mangurian

John Pennington/The Picture Cube

Rich Brommer

Review

family	lower class	middle class
godparents	upper class	women's rights
social class	"nouveaux riches"	

4

How do Latin Americans view life?
How do these views influence the
life styles and activities of Latin
Americans?

A View of Life

The Latin American culture is complex. Like most cultures, it is not always what others think it to be. A Cuban poet, Roberto Fernandez Retamar, wrote the poem which follows for a friend from Europe. In the first part of the poem, the poet talks of the traits his friend sees in him. He paints a picture of himself as seen through the eyes of someone from a different culture. In the second part of the poem, the poet explains how things really are. The poem points out that each culture, like each person, has its own traits. These traits are not always what another culture thinks they are.

I know you want me to tell you of the tomtom in my blood,
Of the great lustrous jungle where the parrot swoops, screaming,
Of lightning fallen before my eyes
And obatala [African saint] white as snow in fire
(Along with the memories I must have of jet trinkets in my shirt,
    the treasures of a twelve-year-old).
I know, friend, I know you need the savage sap
I can bring you, with a chunk of sun in one hand
And, in the other, the maraca [dice game] only the milky dawn can
    finally silence.
But how can I write you with a busted airconditioner,
In this hotel room, this terrible summer day,
La Habana shining at my feet
Like a necklace, full of loud dusty automobiles,
With dozens of restaurants and bars and not a palm in sight?

"A Cuban Writes to a Decidedly European Friend," in José Donoso and William A. Henkin (eds.), *The TriQuarterly Anthology of Contemporary Latin American Literature* (New York: E. P. Dutton & Co., Inc., 1969), p. 111.

BACKGROUND

Individualism, pride, honor, and social status all are very important to Latin Americans. Below, an anthropologist talks about the role some of these play in day-to-day life in Latin America.

Latin Americans are in general sensitive of their "pride" and conscious of "face." Most professional men, executives, and technicians are careful not to perform tasks that they feel are below their position. To do so would endanger their status and might cause them to lose face. A professor feels that he must keep a proper distance from his students for fear that being close would lower him in their eyes. Latin Americans find it amusing when they are told that professional men in the United States help their wives with the dishes; they feel that such a task has no dignity. The work one does points up one's social class. It also represents a strong sense of human dignity. An official of a small town may be offended, feeling that he has not been shown the proper respect, if he is not paid an early formal visit. A secretary in an office may feel hurt if she is asked to dust (not to clean) her employer's desk. A foreman on a plantation can be offended by being asked to perform a job usually done by his workman. Even a poor peasant may feel a loss of face if one appears in his home in response to an invitation to a meal without one's suitcoat. He may feel that the occasion was not considered of enough importance to dress as one might dress for a more important person.

Latin Americans have a very strong sense of what is and is not correct, what will and will not offend. This is reflected in their manners, which often express sentiment. A man will not hesitate to embrace a male friend he has not seen for some time. Every time he meets a friend or an acquaintance, he will shake hands. Often upon meeting a woman, he may bow or kiss her hand. These formal manners often give way to a more informal set of manners when Latin Americans are with family or close friends. Latin Americans think of friends in a special way. Friends are not just people they know fairly well. Instead, friends are people in whom they have complete confidence.

What are some common Latin American character traits? How are these traits interrelated?

How would you compare the Latin American definition of a friend with your own definition?

Adapted from Charles Wagley, *The Latin American Tradition* (New York: Columbia University Press, 1968), pp. 76–77.

Sports, Fun, and Games . . . At one time, bullfighting was considered the national pastime of Latin America. In recent years, this is no longer the case. In Brazil, for example, *futebol,* or soccer, is the national passion. It is a common ground for most Brazilians. In 1970, Brazil became the first country ever to win the world soccer championship three times. Every village has some kind of soccer field, and the larger cities have huge stadiums. In Rio de Janeiro, the soccer stadium can seat over 220,000 fans. While soccer comes first with most Brazilians, they excel in many other sports too, as indicated below.

Happiness is a soccer match, as far as lively, sociable Roberto Leite is concerned. He goes every Saturday afternoon, and his father takes him on Wednesday nights when his grades are up to par. . . .

Blond, nine-year-old Ronaldo often plays with his older brother Roberto. But "they usually end up quarreling," remarks their mother. Together the boys sprawl on their stomachs on the livingroom rug playing "Button Soccer," making their moves on a board as in checkers. . . .

Tennis is another top sport among athletic Brazilians. Young Thomas Koch of Brazil, Mr. Leite pointed out, was one of the best tennis players in the world. Maria Ester Bueno won the U.S. and British tennis championship four times. . . .

Brazil has twice won the world basketball championship in recent years. The *paulistas*, lacking an ice-rink, have been playing hockey on rollerskates. One of their most unusual sports events, however, is the New Year's Eve international footrace through the maze of streets in downtown São Paulo.

Runners from many countries participate every year in this São Silvestre Race. . . . Beginning before midnight, the runners "race into the New Year."

"Bowling is a new sport here that is taking Brazil by storm," remarked Mr. Leite.

"Surfing is very popular too—although dangerous," said the boys' mother.

"But a nice way to die," added Roberto with a wink.

Latin Americans always have been great sports fans. Soccer is the most popular spectator sport. An important game is sometimes taken as seriously as a country's political and economic problems.

*Sergio Larrain
for Magnum*

In Venezuela, on the other hand, a sport that draws large crowds is *beisbol*, or baseball. One visitor to Venezuela described the sport in the following manner.

> . . . [Large] crowds turn up at the *beisbol* park, where Venezuelans watch off-season North American major leaguers. . . . I opted for small fry over the superstars and attended an evening game between two teams of eager 9-year-olds.
>
> I had barely settled into my seat when *bate* met *pelota* with a resounding crack, and the crowd leaped to its feet. It was definitely a *batazo*, good for extra bases. Sure enough, the runner slid into home plate just ahead of the throw, and the crowd shouted, *"¡Jonrón, jonrón!"* The language of beisbol is an intricate marriage of Spanish and English. The losing team, for example, had adopted the name of the Mets of New York, but spelled it *Mezz* in Spanish, which is pronounced *Mess*—a name that admittedly loses something in the translation.

There are other forms of recreation in Latin America. Some of these are depicted in the following illustrations.

Noel Grove, "Venezuela's Crisis of Wealth," *National Geographic*, Vol. 150, No. 2 (August 1976), p. 184.

Rich Brommer

Robert Hatton

Robert Hatton

Scott Seegers © 1967

What are some of the more common forms of recreation in Latin America? How are they similar to or different from yours?

In your opinion, do these serve any other purpose than sheer enjoyment? If so, what?

H. Grathwohl for Alpha Photo Associates, Inc.

A Mexican *fiesta* is a happy event, filled with music, dancing, and bright, colorful costumes.

Living Life to the Fullest . . . Most Latin Americans agree that in order to live life fully, one must feel deeply and strongly about a person or an idea. But they have managed to combine with this the idea that one should enjoy life today and think about tomorrow when it comes. There are many reasons for this attitude. One reason has to do with physical conditions. For example, many poor people believe that they will never escape poverty. They see no reason to save for a rainy day because, for them, every day is a rainy day. Another reason for this attitude has to do with the geographical location. Much of Latin America is in the tropics. In these areas, food must be bought daily and eaten right away or it will spoil. Still another reason relates to the economy. Many Latin American nations are not yet stable economically. When inflation increases, money is worth less. As a result, many feel that the longer savings sit in a bank, the less they are worth. For this reason, some Latin Americans feel that it is wiser to spend their money than to save it.

Perhaps because of these attitudes, Latin America often is thought of as a land of continuous *fiestas* or parties. The *fiestas,* however, do not occur very often, and, as one author explains, they serve a purpose.

. . . the portrait of the Mexican would be incomplete if one were to forget his need for celebrations. . . . Out of the 365 days in the year 120 are holidays in the Mexican calendar. . . . the Mexican has kept intact the art of celebrating. Whether a religious or profane holiday, everything is [an excuse] for public rejoicing. . . .

Holidays are the Mexican peasant's only luxury. They are [essential] for they allow him to come out of himself, to open up. On those days the silent Mexican shouts, sings, lights firecrackers, eats and drinks too much, fires his pistol. Sometimes in the air, sometimes at his brother. He also discharges his soul. . . . It is not a question of earning the benedictions or good graces of a patron saint or God. . . . It is rather a free offering, an affirmation of strength and health.

There are many kinds of *fiestas.* Some are held in small villages. Others go on for several days and draw crowds of fascinated tourists from all over the world. One of the most famous *fiestas* is Carnival, which marks the beginning of the Christian Lenten season. Carnival is celebrated throughout Latin America. But the most famous celebration, described below, takes place in Brazil.

All year long as the "Cariocas" of Rio de Janeiro work and go to school, they look forward to one three-day holiday—Carnival. Men, women, and children save their *cruzeiros* (the Brazilian money) to buy a costume for this event. . . .

Carnival is a time for dancing in the streets, parades, fancy dress balls, and general gaiety. . . .

There are many Carnival clubs and teams which compete to win prizes for the best dancing, the best songs and music composed especially for the Carnival, the best costumes, and the most beautiful and original floats. Sometimes the costumes . . . are made of costly silks and satins, and represent lords and ladies of the empire days, and sometimes the costumes are only meant to be funny.

As the day for Carnival draws near, everyone in Rio is excited. Millions of packages of confetti are sold, and so are "serpentines," long, thin strips of colored paper rolled into tight, round disks. When

André Camp, *The Mexico I Love,* trans. Ruth Whipple Fermaud (New York: Tudor Publishing Company, 1968), pp. 93–96.

From *The First Book of Brazil,* pp. 67–70, by Sally Sheppard, copyright 1962 by Franklin Watts, Inc.

a person holds one end of the paper and throws the disk, it unravels into a long streamer. Almost everyone buys a mask. . . . Sometimes the masks are huge, grotesque heads made of papier-mâché.

A few days before Carnival, every household in Rio is busy putting last-minute touches to costumes and planning parties and dances. Children and grownups alike buy horns and other noisemakers. Carnival clubs hold final rehearsals in the hope that their entries will win the prizes. Preparations are all very secret. . . .

In Rio the festivities open at noon on Saturday. Until the following Wednesday everything stops for the three-day holiday.

On Sunday night, large groups known as the "samba schools" parade in costume. They have their own bands and have made up songs and music which they play for the judges. On Monday night the "ranchos," which are similar but small groups, parade. The music of the "ranchos" is sadder and slower than the gay rhythms of the "samba schools." Tuesday, the last night of Carnival, is the most exciting and colorful of all. It is then that the huge floats and decorated automobiles drive slowly through the city in a parade that seems endless.

By Wednesday morning, Carnival is over and the streets are almost deserted except for the street cleaners, who are busy gathering up the tons of confetti and the miles of paper serpentines.

The *fiesta* is one way Latin Americans express the desire to relax and enjoy life. The *siesta* is another. For years, business and other such matters have been put aside for a few hours in the middle of the workday. It is a time to relax. People try to go home to enjoy a good meal, take a *siesta*, or nap, and just take it easy. In recent years, however, the old Spanish custom of the *siesta* is undergoing changes. Many industries cannot afford to shut down their assembly lines for two or three hours each day. Cities have become larger. People live farther away from their jobs. Urban transportation systems are hard put to withstand the burden put on them by people rushing home for the *siesta*. Many Latin Americans in large urban areas feel that the trip home has become too hectic. They prefer to spend their *siesta* time with friends near their place of work. But, even in the places where the custom of the *siesta* is changing or disappearing, Latin Americans have not changed their eating habits. Their noon meal is still eaten at one or two o'clock in the afternoon. A light supper is eaten after nine o'clock in the evening.

What are some of the reasons for the Latin American attitude of "Enjoy life today, and worry about tomorrow when it comes"? How does this attitude compare with the one found in your country?

Why are *fiestas* important to the Latin Americans?

What is the purpose of the *siesta*? Why is the custom changing or dying out? Would you like a *siesta* time? Why or why not?

When It Comes to Dying . . . A famous Peruvian poet once wrote:

What is living? To dream without sleeping.
What is dying? To sleep without dreaming.
Many Latin Americans share this attitude. They accept, or are resigned to, death. Others do not share that quiet acceptance. Two different views are expressed below. The first is the statement of an elderly Mexican. He lives in a country village. The second is the reaction of a young woman to her aunt's death. She lives in the city.

Well, life is coming to a close. I am an old man now. I have come a long way and death is all that awaits me. What a pity that I am going to leave my beautiful hills! But I am resigned to it. My race is over, the mission God has given me is fulfilled. I have folded the page. Good or bad, I was what I was. Now I want nothing more, except perhaps another wife, just to bury me.

I am thankful to God that I have lived. I have raised my children and taught them the little I know. My responsibility is over. . . .

I can no longer think of trying to improve myself, of studying or learning something new, especially now that my sight is beginning to fail. I guess there is good reason why I tire. . . . But, of course, I will always go on being upright. An old man has no energy left for other things.

Oscar Lewis, *Pedro Martínez: A Mexican Peasant and His Family* (New York: Random House, Inc., 1964), pp. 457–458.

What can I say to express the pain that has drained away the last drop of joy from my heart? I have never been able to accept death the way it comes to people in my class. We are all going to die, yes, but why in such inhuman, miserable conditions? I've always thought there was no need for the poor to die like that. Their struggle is so tremendous . . . so titantic . . . no, no, it isn't fair. They can be saved. I refuse to resign myself to death in that tragic form.

There are authors who have written that the Mexican cares nothing about life and knows how to face death. There are jokes and sayings and songs about it but I would like to see those famous writers in our place, undergoing the terrible, hideous sufferings we do, and then see if they are able to accept the death of any one of us . . . knowing that the person didn't have to die. . . . The way I see it, there's nothing charming about death nor is it something we have become accustomed to because we celebrate *fiestas* for the dead. . . .

Oscar Lewis, *A Death in the Sanchez Family* (New York: Random House, Inc., 1969), p. 35.

What attitude does the old man have toward life and death? How do you know he feels that way?

What attitude does the young woman have toward death? About what is she so angry and bitter? How does her attitude compare with the old man's? In your opinion, how are their attitudes influenced by their age? By their social status?

Do you think these attitudes are common only to Latin Americans? Why or why not?

EXPLORATION

Machismo, or *hombría*, is very much a part of Latin American life. The only group not much influenced by it is the Indians. *Machismo* can be shown through political leadership or literary efforts. Being *macho* can mean being a ladies' man.

It can mean caring about good manners and having a lot of self-confidence. As noted below, *machismo* means something a little different to different people.

> "*To be* macho *is to be a man, a real one.*"

> "*The essense of* machismo *is valor, and a valiant man, is one who is strong and tough, who is able to defend himself and his family, who doesn't seek fights but who doesn't dodge them if forced upon him.*"

> "*Concern with face and dignity, and sensitivity to public opinion appear to be a part of* machismo.*"

> *People are reluctant to name* machos. *In answer to direct questions they usually reply, "Now there are no longer* machos; *we are all the same.*"

> "*I would never give up or say, 'Enough,' even though the other was killing me. I would try to go to my death smiling. That is what we mean by being 'macho,' by being manly.*"

How is *machismo* reflected in the everyday attitudes and behavior of most Latin Americans?

Does the Latin American view of life described in this chapter contradict the statement, "Now there are no longer *machos; we are all the same*"? Explain your answer.

Do people in your society have a strong feeling for *machismo?* Explain your answer.

In what ways, if any, is the Latin American view of life different from yours? If it is different, what do you think causes it to be that way?

Review

character traits
fiestas
Carnival

siesta
recreation

death
machismo

5

What factors have shaped the religious life of Latin America?

How do Latin Americans view religion?

The Sword and the Cross

They brought me in at New Year's to take the oath as fiscal [village official]. One of the oldest men in the village was my yajualtiquil [the elder in an Indian village who advises the religious and political authorities]. After I took the oath we went to the church and he taught me about the saints. . . .

Then he pointed to Santiago and said, "This is the patron saint of animals. The men and women who own mules or horses ask him to take care of them. They light candles to him on Friday because Friday is the day of the animals.

"This next is San Miguel, the patron saint of musicians. He's the chief of the harps and guitars, and the musicians pray to him because they have to play day and night at fiestas and funerals and he keeps them awake. They also ask him to take care of their wives so nothing will happen to them. . . .

"This saint in the coffin is San Manuel. He's also called San Salvador or San Mateo. He watches over the people. They ask him to watch over them when they're at home or in their fields or on the road. . . .

"This next one is the patron saint of the church. His name is San Juan Evangelista. He was the first person to plant a cornfield. He was the first man in the world. He was born before Jesus Christ. He cleared the scrub off the mountains and taught the people to live the way they do today. At each fiesta the people ask him for good health so they can get their work done."

Catholicism is the main religion of Latin America. Yet it is more than a religion. It is a way of life. The crosses and small chapels that dot the countryside are evidence of the importance of the Catholic faith. Today, as in the past, each village has a patron saint. Many even bear the name of that saint. Everyone joins in the festivities to honor the village's saint. Each family and family member also has a patron saint. So do various groups, such as truck drivers, labor unions, and childless wives. The church is so much a part of everyday life in Latin America that many people who do not even attend services consider themselves faithful Catholics.

Ricardo Pozas, *Juan the Chamula*, trans. Lysander Kemp (Berkeley: University of California Press, 1962), pp. 92–96. Copyright 1962 by The Regents of the University of California; reprinted by permission of the University of California Press.

The influence of Catholicism in Latin America goes back to the conquest of the New World by the Spanish, for with the sword came the cross. The priests represented the church. They worked to convert the Indians to Christianity. They took care of the spiritual needs of the Spanish and Portuguese settlers. When the African slaves arrived, they tended them, too.

In order to serve everyone's needs, priests had to carry their religion outside their churches and missions. Religion became a part of all aspects of community life. A passage across a mountain that was not safe was marked by a cross or a small chapel. Each ranch had its own chapel. Each village, group, and family had its own patron saint. Even the church bell had a role. It rang out the start and finish of each day. The Church was the only institution which gave the people schools, hospitals, orphanages, and welfare services.

Much of the Catholic Church's power and wealth came from its close ties with the government. In the New World empires, both the Spanish and the Portuguese rulers were the heads of religious, as well as political, life. Their status was accepted by the pope. Church leaders played an important part in almost everything that happened. Great wealth was acquired through favors from the State and offerings from faithful worshipers. The Church received many large pieces of land in this way. There also were large profits from the Church's many business interests, such as ranching, farming, commerce, mining, and banking.

What was the role of the Catholic Church in the colonial era? Why did it become so powerful?

During colonial times in Latin America, life often centered around the local church.

Organization of American States

The National Period . . . When the fight for independence came, the Church leaders backed the European powers. After the Latin Americans had won their independence, the new political leaders began to question the Church's power. They were joined by anticlericals, people who felt that the Church had too much social, economic, and political power. The anticlericals were not anti-Catholic. In fact, most of them were Catholics. Their main goal was to limit the Church to religious matters and bring it under the control of the State. They felt that the Church should be less worldly and more spiritual.

One of the anticlericals' main concerns was the Church's large landholdings. Some of them wanted to acquire Church lands for their own use. Others felt that so much land in the hands of one institution was unfair to society. In Mexico, for example, before land reform became law, the Church owned one half of the most valuable land. Church laws did not allow the sale of its property. This greatly reduced the amount of land the people could have. The anticlericals had other concerns, too. Church lands and businesses did not have to pay taxes. The anticlericals felt that this gave the Church an advantage. They also felt that it deprived the government of badly needed funds.

Bit by bit, the anticlericals made their reforms. The Church lost many of its property holdings. Many of its business activities were cut back, too. Because of this, the Church lost much of its wealth and was left short of money.

What was anticlericalism? What did the anticlericals want? What effect did they have on the Catholic Church?

The Catholic Church Today . . . The influence of the Church has decreased since 1900. The State has taken over some of the duties that used to fall to the Church. For example, to be legal, there must be a civil, as well as a religious marriage ceremony. Today, the State, not the Church, takes care of most of the educational, health, and welfare services. And, in most places, religious instruction is not allowed in public school.

About one half of the Latin American countries have ordered the separation of Church and State. Still, the Church is not completely removed from politics. Though members of the clergy no longer hold public office, many will take a public stand when the issues involve matters of faith. Since the late 1950's, the Church has changed many of its views. During colonial times, it tended to go along with views that would allow it to keep its privileged position. Today, for the most part, it goes along with the cause of reform.

One of the clergy's main goals is agrarian reform, a more equal division of land among the people. Priests have begun to organize credit unions and cooperatives. Such groups buy and sell at fair prices for members. Church lay people are forming Christian labor unions and political parties. These groups point out the need for social justice in keeping with Catholic teachings and democratic principles.

In 1968, Pope Paul VI visited Colombia. He was the first pope to visit Latin America. In a speech he made in Bogotá, he told those who had gathered to listen that the Church understood and backed their desire for reform.

> We know your living conditions: they are, for many of you, miserable, often below the normal needs of human living. We cannot forget about you. We wish to be a sharer in your good cause, which is that of poor people.
>
> We know how in Latin America economic and social development has not been equal. It has favored those who first promoted it, it has passed over the many native peoples.
>
> We know that today you notice the low level of your conditions, and that you are impatient to get a more just distribution of goods and a better recognition of your numbers and your proper place in society. And we think that you have some awareness of the defense of your lot undertaken by the church.
>
> But today the question has become serious, because you have become aware of your needs and pain, and you cannot tolerate that your conditions should last forever and not change at once.
>
> We then ask ourself what we can do for you.
>
> We will continue to defend your cause.

The Church's political efforts are not effective all the time. In some Latin American countries, divorce laws have been passed. In others, there are birth control programs. Yet, neither divorce nor birth control are in line with Catholic teachings. The Church's work for agrarian reforms has not always met with success either. Some people feel that the reforms backed by the Church will lead to socialism or communism.

One of the main reasons the Church's influence is not as strong as it used to be is its lack of priests and funds. There are 50 million more people in Latin America today than there were fifteen years ago. But there are only twelve thousand more priests. This means that there is one priest for every six thousand Catholics. In the United States, for example, there is one for every seven hundred Catholics.

The lack of funds is just as serious as the lack of priests. Most of the magnificent churches, artwork, and altars date back to the times before the Church lost its wealth. Catholic churches in Western Europe and the United

States are providing financial help and sending priests to Latin America. Despite this, there are still too few clergy, too little money, and too much to be done.

In what ways has the influence of the Church decreased since 1900? What are some of the reasons for the decrease?

What is the Church's role in agrarian reform? How does it differ from its past role? What, if anything, does this indicate about the attitudes of the Church?

The Roman Catholic Church was both a religious and social center. Many of the religious holidays, festivals, and saints' days are still celebrated today with processions such as this one.

The Protestants . . . About 10 percent of the Latin American people are Protestant. When the Latin American countries were still Spanish and Portuguese colonies, non-Catholics were not welcome. Although this changed after the Spanish and Portuguese power fell, it was not until the 1900's that the number of Protestants began to grow. Protestant missionaries have had a lot to do with much of this growth. The missionaries, who have worked to help both the urban and rural low-income groups, have built hospitals, schools, and colleges. They have gained a great many followers, especially in Brazil.

There are many reasons why Protestantism has grown so slowly in Latin America. The main one, however, stems from the fact that the Catholic religion is so much a part of daily life for most Latin Americans. For this reason, the Latin American Catholics who become Protestants are changing more than just their religion. In some ways, they have to change their life styles, too. And, in some cases, conversion can put a strain on family ties and friendships as well.

Why has Protestantism grown so slowly in Latin America?

In your opinion, how could being a Protestant affect a person's way of life in Latin America? Why might it have such an effect?

A Combination of Faiths . . .

Many Latin American Indians and blacks are Catholics. In a lot of cases, however, their Catholicism is closely mixed in with their own age-old religious beliefs and customs. Those who practice this combination of faiths feel that they are true Catholics. The two accounts which follow are about this mixture.

David Mangurian

In Guatemala

I first visited the cathedral on Maundy Thursday [the Thursday of the Holy Week before Easter]. As I was about to leave, I saw a small group of Indians disappear down some steep steps which led under the cathedral floor. I followed them into a low-roofed, dark little crypt where candles burned before a cross. They and their forefathers had been lighting candles there for so long that the walls and roof were blackened with soot. So, too, was the cross before which the Indians now silently prayed.

A few minutes earlier they had been saying prayers before the crucifix in the ruined cathedral. Now they prayed some special prayers before a special cross. For in this one, they believed, dwelt a spirit to whom due honor must also be paid.

Over lunch a priest told me that that same morning one of his best lay catechists [unordained teacher of religion] had gone straight from serving Mass to lead a band of pilgrims to a figureless cross high up in the hills. There he led them in prayer. It was not to the God whom the Spaniards had brought to them 500 years ago that he and the other Indians had prayed, but to the spirit of the mountain whose cult went back far into the past and who, they believed, dwelt within this part-pagan, part-Christian symbol. . . .

In many parts of Guatemala the Indians have erected their own crosses on which there is no figure of Christ. These crosses are frequently placed in spots where a nature spirit is believed to dwell. Often, when mission priests have brought an Indian community to the point where they believe the people now to be Christianized, they ask them . . . to get rid of the crosses they possess so that these may be replaced by crucifixes. . . .

Douglas Hyde, *The Troubled Continent* (Dayton, Ohio: Pflaum Press, 1967), pp. 23–24.

In Brazil

The oddest and probably the most typical church in Bahia [a province in northern Brazil] is Nosso Senhor do Bomfim. It is a church for the black people, and is the center of a cult which is a strange mixture of Christian and old African rites. Here you meet with the magic word that crops up wherever the old Africa breaks through the crust of Afro-Brazil. In Rio de Janeiro the word is *macumba*, in Recife *xangô*, and in Bahia *candomblé*. The name refers to the magic of the Brazilian blacks which is a lot like the witchcraft and magic cults of the Caribbean. In Bahia, 30 percent of the black people are supposed to be followers of candomblé. There are even a few whites who say they believe in these rites of old Africa, and their number is said to be growing.

The Catholic Church tries to hold back candomblé by both gentle and strong methods. In this struggle, both parties have had to give in in many ways. The clergy has to shut its eyes to a good many things. On the other hand, candomblé followers have had to give their African gods the disguise of Christian names. The African goddess of the sea and fertility, Yêmanja, became the Virgin Mary. The thunder god Xangô was renamed St. Anthony. The sky god Olorun became God the Father, and Ogun, the good god of light, Jesus Christ. Finally, the wicked demon Exú put on the mask of the Christian devil.

In Nosso Senhor do Bomfim, Christianized candomblé has been almost legalized. Believers come there to pray for health, happiness, and a better way of life. They also try to bargain with their god for miracles. Old African black magic is being born again under a cloak of Christianity. The prayers in this church are very human, very childlike, and very pagan. So are the gruesomely realistic offerings, the plaster babies, flaming hearts, pictures of operation scars, X-ray pictures of dental abscesses.

A Bahian group of artists painted thanksgiving pictures in oil for the church. Construction workers who fell from skyscrapers offer thanks for being miraculously saved. Criminals praise the church for helping them escape the police.

The church is also a colorful African bazaar. Peddlers and beggars swarm in front of and inside the building. They hold out their hands, sell

Manchete from Pictorial Parade

amulets, candles, and plaster casts. The noisy commercial activity reaches its peak when the festival of cleaning of the church begins. That is the grandest, most splendid religious festival in Bahia. On the day of the washing, fireworks are set off everywhere in the province. Processions come from far away on foot or by boat. Drums throb, there is dancing in the streets, and thousands of people carry jugs and tubs of water into the church to clean it as their ancestors cleaned African temples of evil spirits.

Why do you think ancient Indian and African religious practices have continued to exist?

In what ways have the Indians and the blacks made Christianity fit their own needs?

Are the Indian and African approaches to Catholicism at all alike? Explain your answer.

Why might Indians and blacks who continue to follow ancient beliefs still consider themselves good Catholics?

EXPLORATION

Four Latin American Catholics were asked the question, "What do you believe about religion?" They answered as follows:

"I am Catholic, a child of God, but I don't go to the Church. Most priests only fool the people into giving them money. But for what? Have you ever seen how most priests live? I say, if the priests use the money to help the needy, I will respect them. My woman says I shouldn't talk like this, that God will punish me.

"I asked my woman what the Church ever did for her. She says it gives her faith to accept what happens as the will of God. I prefer to believe in the powers of the angels outside the Church. I also pray to Padre Cicero. Now there was a priest who gave to the poor, who helped the poor man in his struggles. But what did the Church think of him? Did the Church welcome a true saint of the people? No, they refused to keep him in the Church.

"Padre Cicero is my patron saint. . . . He loved people so much that miracles still happen among those who come here on pilgrimages to where he lived and preached. I have his picture in my home and wear his image on a chain around my neck. Since I started wearing it I have never been struck by malaria or smallpox or any bad disease. I put a Padre Cicero medal on each of my children. . . ."

"My Uncle Alfredo is a religious man. . . . He belongs to the Men's Circle in the church. Every Good Friday he helps carry the platform bearing Our Savior through the streets. I don't get involved. My father told me he had me baptized, but . . . we never went to Mass. Father would take us in the processions honoring his patron saint, Padre Cicero. He made us all wear Padre Cicero medals. I still wear mine, mainly out of respect for my father. . . . Well, I don't believe in Padre Cicero, but the medal can't do any harm either.

"For myself, I believe a man needs faith. Without faith that God and the Saints were watching over him, man would be alone and without hope. I count myself as a Christian even though I don't go to the church. After all, going to church is mostly for the women, girls, and older men."

"I am Catholic. Every Sunday I go to Mass and sometimes I go on weekday mornings at six o'clock too. I pray mostly to Our Holy Mother asking for guidance in raising my children. I always feel relieved after I've been to Mass. It's difficult to explain what peace and strength my faith gives me to face the day. I believe religion is essential to everyone's life. If they only knew how much they could receive from God's grace, they would practice their faith more."

"I go to Mass occasionally, but I'm not what you'd call a devout Catholic. Don't misunderstand. I do believe in God and want to practice the Commandments. I just don't feel I have to go to Church to practice my beliefs."

Rosemary G. Messick, *Brazil: Focus on Rising Expectations* (Englewood Cliffs, New Jersey: Prentice-Hall, Inc., 1975), pp. 67–69.

In what ways, if any, do these views help explain the strength of the Catholic Church in Latin America?

In what ways, if any, do these views illustrate why religion is a vital part of everyday life in Latin America?

Review

Catholicism
the Church
anticlericals

Pope Paul VI
Protestantism
Indian Catholicism

black Catholicism
candomblé

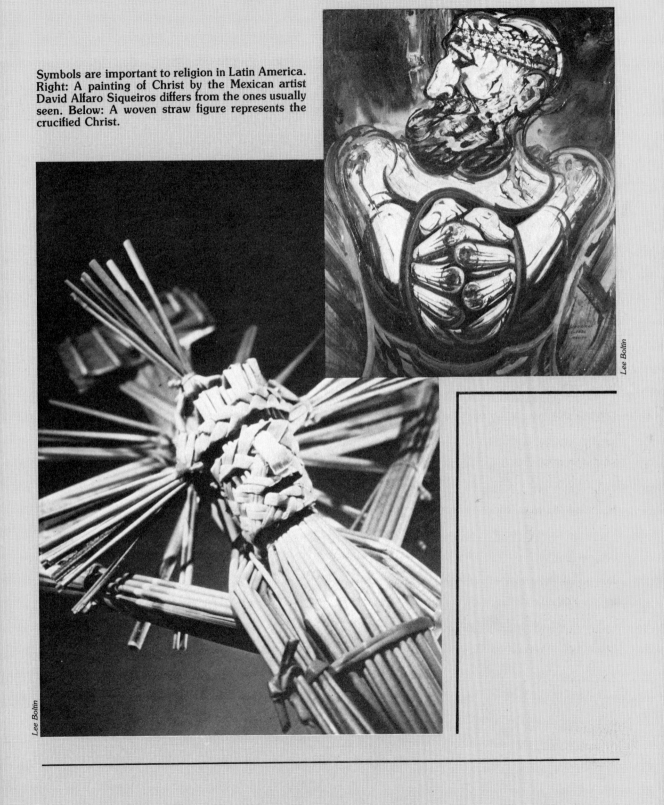

Symbols are important to religion in Latin America. Right: A painting of Christ by the Mexican artist David Alfaro Siqueiros differs from the ones usually seen. Below: A woven straw figure represents the crucified Christ.

6

What is school like in Latin America?

How well does education in Latin America meet the needs of the people?

The Need to Learn

Education is an important issue in Latin America today. For too long a time, too many Latin Americans could not read or write. The poor could not afford to go to school. Today, public education is free in most of Latin America. Still, there remains much to be done in the field of education. As explained below, as yet there are not enough schools or teachers for the rapidly growing number of Latin Americans.

In all three countries [Peru, Bolivia, Ecuador] some schools are so overcrowded that students must attend in shifts. In many areas there is a morning shift, an afternoon shift, and an evening one, with classes lasting only about half an hour. . . .

Away from the capitals and other large cities teachers may be too scarce to permit shifts. During the first weeks of the school year students crowd into the classrooms until some must sit on windowsills or perhaps the teacher's table. Up to eighty may crowd into a room meant for a third that number. Before long, the high drop-out rate . . . cuts down the attendance. . . . Eventually the classes contain twenty-five to forty students—still too many, but that's quite usual in South America. . . .

Country schools are usually elementary schools. For additional education, the student goes to a town or other urban center. When he starts high school, a student may carry up to eighteen courses. . . . Students usually buy their own texts. . . . Only wealthy families can afford many texts, so most schools manage without them. The teacher has a text and a manual from which he reads lessons that the students copy down. Few schools have libraries to which pupils can go to check anything they miss in class. . . . Getting educated amounts to a great deal of memorizing of the notes one takes.

Reprinted by permission of the Publisher, Thomas Nelson, Inc. From the book *Peru, Bolivia, Ecuador: The Indian Andes*, pp. 153–154, 161. Copyright © 1969 by Charles Paul May.

Efforts are being made in most of Latin America to improve education. But progress is slow. There are many problems to be overcome. One problem stems from the fact that in most Latin American countries, public education is controlled by the national governments. Most decisions are made by ministers of education. They decide where and when to build schools, what courses are to be taught, and what books are to be used. They also make decisions about the hiring of teachers. Many of the ministers are appointed. They have little or no experience as educators. The ministers have short terms of office. At times, this means that policy changes are frequent and confusing.

Another problem is that there are not enough teachers. One reason for this is that there is little prestige in teaching. Another reason is the low pay. It is not unheard of for an urban teacher to take an extra job to make enough money to meet living expenses. The position of the rural teacher is even worse. Life in the country does not hold the excitement of city life. Often it also does not have such urban comforts as plumbing and electricity. As a result, it is not easy to get teachers to move to rural areas.

It is estimated that only one half of Latin America's teachers have teaching degrees. Most of the trained teachers are found in the urban areas. In the country, many teachers have only a grade school education. Because of this, most students are taught to memorize their lessons. The teacher dictates the lesson, and the student writes it down and learns it. Questions and creative thinking are not encouraged.

What are some of the reasons for the teacher shortage?

What are some of the other problems facing education in Latin America?

The Latin American Schools . . . Latin American children usually start school at the age of six or seven. They spend about six years in grade school and six in secondary school. The final step is college.

Most of the schools emphasize subjects such as languages, the arts, literature, and philosophy. In the past, school was mainly for children of the upper class. In recent years, however, an effort has been made to meet the needs of children from low-income families. There are more and different courses being offered. The grade schools teach reading, writing, math, cleanliness, prevention of disease, and farming. In the higher grades, there is a new emphasis on such modern subjects as the physical and social sciences. But, the main reason for the secondary school remains the same—to prepare students for college studies.

Public education now is required in most Latin American countries, and the number of schools is increasing. These children attend a school in Managua, Nicaragua.

The public schools in Latin America differ from area to area. But most of the newer ones are like the Venezuelan one described below.

A typical secondary school is the Liceo Lino de Clemente. Located near the eastern end of the Caracas valley, it was built of cement block in the early 1960's. Eight classrooms and four laboratories rise around three sides of a central auditorium, all under a sloping roof that lets in light and air. On the fourth side the auditorium is open to the outdoors, with walks leading to basketball and volleyball courts. The classrooms have outside windows, but no doors in the inner doorways. This gives an open feel, though things get noisy when every classroom is in use.

The school was meant for about 300 boys and girls from two areas, one well-to-do, the other rather poor. All students wear the same neat uniform. For the boys this is khaki slacks and short-sleeved shirts with black shoes or sneakers; for the girls, white jumpers over blue blouses with white socks and dark moccasins or sneakers. Such uniforms are standard in Venezuelan public schools, though they cannot always be had in rural areas.

Classes run from eight to eleven in the morning and two to five in the afternoon, five days a week. The break is the traditional siesta. Once a week the morning class periods end with a meeting in the auditorium, really a talk on some civic or historic topic.

The students, who are in age from eleven to seventeen, take subjects like those in the United States junior-high and high schools. They include Spanish grammar and literature, English, history, civics, mathematics, and science. Most of the teachers are men.

Adapted from *Hello Venezuela*, p. 118, by Morris Weeks, Jr. Copyright © 1968. Used by permission of Grosset & Dunlap, Inc.

Because of educational reforms, more Latin American children are able to go to school. This is a tenth grade algebra class for children of Bolivian miners.

David Mangurian

The situation in the private schools is not so very different. There are a great many private schools in Latin America. Of these, a good number are church schools. Still, in most cases, the private schools are ruled by the same ministries of education as the public schools. In the reading which follows, a young Chilean talks about school.

The school that I went to was in Santiago, the capital of Chile. It went up to the eighth grade. All the students were from the middle class. My parents paid a $10.00 entrance fee at the beginning of the school year and a tuition fee of $1.00 for each month that I was in school. I had to buy my own textbooks. Most of the money to run the school came from the government.

Our school was a large building, like the schools in the United States. So were our classrooms. We had bulletin boards, blackboards, and other kinds of equipment. Two students shared a *banco*, a desk attached to the floor. All the students wore a uniform—black pants, white shirt, blue tie, and blue blazer. There were about 2,000 boys in the school. There were no girls.

Since I lived only a quarter of a mile from school, I walked. But students who came from farther away would ride the bus or be brought in a car. Some schools had school buses, but most students took the public buses.

Adapted from an Interview with Douglas Azocar, Chilean exchange student, La Habra, California.

We went to school from the end of March to the end of November. Our summer vacation lasted from December to February, which is the summer season in Chile. We had a week off in September to celebrate Chilean independence. We also had time off around Christmas, a two-week vacation in August, and about twenty patriotic holidays.

About 60 students were in my class. Until the seventh grade, one teacher taught all the subjects. But in the higher grades one teacher taught one subject. The students stayed in one room, and the teachers moved from room to room.

We went to school from 8 in the morning until 12:30. We had five periods with a break after the second. After the fifth period, we went home, and another group of students came. They went to school from 1 to 7. We had to have two shifts because there were so many students.

In most schools in Chile, our marks were in numbers. The best mark was a 7. Anything below a 4 was not passing. We had three big tests each year. If you didn't pass them, you failed. The tests were made by the government and were about one hour long. The tests were mostly essay, but there were some true and false questions. During the year each teacher would often give one-hour essay tests. Sometimes we had oral tests where we would have to recite answers to the teachers.

What are Latin American schools like? In what ways, if any, are they like the schools with which you are familiar? In what ways, if any, are they different? What benefits, if any, are there in a private school?

David Mangurian

Some Latin American countries are trying to increase the number of vocational schools. This is the interior of an industrial vocational school in Aratu, Brazil.

Vocational Schools . . . One alternative to the regular public school is the vocational school. The aim of this type of school is to train students to be skilled and technical workers. Even though there is a great shortage of such workers, there is not enough financial support for the schools. And the training they offer is often of poor quality.

Some Latin American countries are trying to promote vocational education. The advantages of such an education are illustrated in the reading below about Alicia, a student from a poor family in Brazil.

> Alicia attracted the attention of her teachers because she was a serious and hard-working girl of fifteen years. She was obviously from a poor home, for she wore the same dress to school, night after night. Her father worked [off and on] at unskilled labor, and drank too much. Her mother was in poor health. The large family lived in a hovel [run-down house] next to the railroad. Their main source of income were Alicia's wages as a factory worker and those of her sister.
>
> Working eight hours a day and attending . . . school three hours in the evening, Alicia completed the three-year course in two years. With the assistance of the school, she changed from her factory job to one in an office; and shortly afterward she began work in a bank. She succeeded in her new jobs—partly because in school she had learned to dress better and to get along socially with her teachers and colleagues. She became an attractive and outgoing young woman.
>
> At the age of eighteen Alicia passed a difficult examination for entrance to a higher commercial school in a large city nearby. She completed this course and then qualified for a job with good pay in the government of her home town. Her first act was to move her family into a comfortable apartment in a good part of the town, giving the younger children a chance to attend better schools. Success in secondary school and then in a school of commerce gave Alicia a self-assurance that enabled her to move easily among middle-class people.

But there are not enough stories such as Alicia's. Less than 40 percent of the students take such courses as industrial arts, home economics, and farming. There are several reasons for this. A child must be twelve or thirteen years old to take part in vocational schooling. By that age, many children of low-income families no longer are in school. Also, such training conflicts with a strong Latin American cultural value—a scornful view of manual labor. Vocational training, and the jobs to which it leads, are too closely related to such labor. Therefore, middle-class students tend to stay away.

Reprinted from *Society and Education in Brazil*, pp. 188–189, by Robert J. Havighurst and Roberto Moreira by permission of the University of Pittsburgh Press. © 1965 by University of Pittsburgh Press.

What is the purpose of vocational education in Latin America? Why, if at all, is this kind of education necessary? Why has it not been more successful?

Do you think that the way Latin Americans look at such training will change in the next few years? Why or why not?

Robert Hatton

The National University of Mexico has more than 100,000 students. Special murals, such as this one, decorate many of the buildings.

A Higher Education . . . The number of colleges and the size of their student bodies have increased greatly during the 1900's. Yet they too are short of money. They can educate only a small part of the people. There is not enough money for library books, equipment, and new buildings. In the last few years, the number of college courses has grown to include the physical sciences, public and business administration, and other such fields. Still, a lot of the students choose such age-old majors as history, literature, law, and medicine. Few plan careers in farming, engineering, or science. Yet it is in such fields that there is the greatest need for skilled people.

The social status of college professors is high, and many take the job mainly for the prestige it offers. Few are full-time teachers. Most spend much of their time on other means of earning a living. College students have a great deal of power. They often dominate the councils that run the schools. Student groups sometimes call strikes to demand administration and faculty changes. Often, the real issues behind such action are political and do not have anything to do with the school. Yet such strikes have gotten in the way of classroom work and forced some schools to close for a while. Because of some of the strikes, schools have had to lower their academic standards.

Do you think that Latin and North American colleges, professors, and students are basically the same? In what ways, if any, do they differ?

Education and the Indian . . . Whether or not to educate the Indians is still a topic for debate in many Latin American countries. Many Indian communities do not want public education because they fear that it will weaken a child's respect for their way of life. In some places, Indians are considered as second-rate citizens not worth schooling. The excerpt which follows is from a novel written in the 1940's, at the time of World War II. It tells of the efforts of the mayor of an Indian village to set up a school.

[Rosendo] Maqui [the mayor] had been authorized by the community to hire a teacher, and after many inquiries he finally got the son of a law clerk from the capital of the province to accept the position. . . . He said to Rosendo:

"You'll need books, slates, pencils, and tablets."

The pencils in the store were very expensive. By making inquiries here and there [Maqui] finally learned that the School Commissioner was supposed to give them the supplies. He found him in a café having a few drinks.

"Come back such and such a day," the commissioner said grudgingly.

Maqui came back on the day he was told, and the official, after listening to his request with raised eyebrows, informed him that he had no supplies on hand at the moment. He would have to order them from Lima and they would probably not get there before next year. The mayor went to the son of the law clerk to tell him what he had learned, and the young fellow answered him:

"So you were in earnest about the school. I thought you were joking. I'm not going to scuffle with wooden-headed Indians for less than fifty soles [Peruvian money]."

Maqui told him he would have to let him know, for he had reported that the salary agreed on was thirty soles. Time went by. The supplies did not arrive the following year. Only then did the commissioner tell him that he would have to send in an application stating the number of pupils and other things. He also said, at this late date, that the community would have to put up a special building. . . . The . . . mayor agreed to everything. He counted the children, and found there were more than a hundred; then he went to a lawyer to have him draw up the petition. It cost him five soles and it was finally sent off. At the same time he got the community to authorize the salary of fifty soles a month to the teacher and he called on several of the villagers, among them those who were the best masons, to build the special house. They began to mix the mud and shape the abodes with hearty enthusiasm.

That was how things stood at the moment. Perhaps there would be a school. If only the supplies came through and the teacher didn't change his mind again. It would be a good thing for the children to know how to read and write. . . .

From *Broad and Alien Is the World,* by Ciro Alegría, pp. 15–17. Translated by Harriet De Onís. Copyright 1941, © 1969 by Holt, Rinehart and Winston. Reprinted by permission of Holt, Rinehart and Winston, Publishers.

In your opinion, what was the general view toward setting up a school in the Indian village? What methods were used to discourage Maqui?

How did Maqui feel about the school? Why was he so persistent?

What problems could develop for the Indians if the school is established? For the non-Indians?

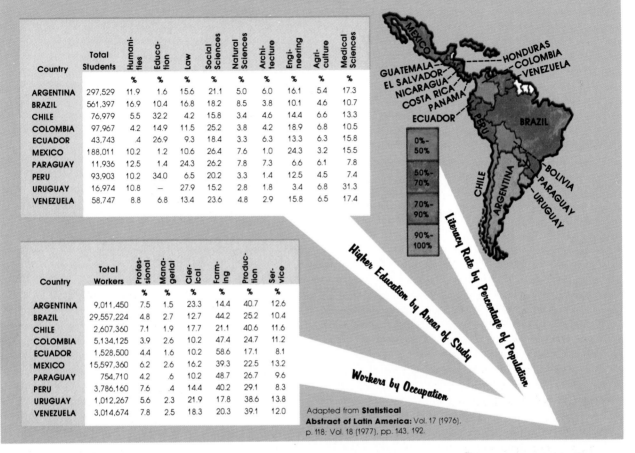

Country	Total Students	Humanities %	Education %	Law %	Social Sciences %	Natural Sciences %	Architecture %	Engineering %	Agriculture %	Medical Sciences %
ARGENTINA	297,529	11.9	1.6	15.6	21.1	5.0	6.0	16.1	5.4	17.3
BRAZIL	561,397	16.9	10.4	16.8	18.2	8.5	3.8	10.1	4.6	10.7
CHILE	76,979	5.5	32.2	4.2	15.8	3.4	4.6	14.4	6.6	13.3
COLOMBIA	97,967	4.2	14.9	11.5	25.2	3.8	4.2	18.9	6.8	10.5
ECUADOR	43,743	.4	26.9	9.3	18.4	3.3	6.3	13.3	6.3	15.8
MEXICO	188,011	10.2	1.2	10.6	26.4	7.6	1.0	24.3	3.2	15.5
PARAGUAY	11,936	12.5	1.4	24.3	26.2	7.8	7.3	6.6	6.1	7.8
PERU	93,903	10.2	34.0	6.5	20.2	3.3	1.4	12.5	4.5	7.4
URUGUAY	16,974	10.8	—	27.9	15.2	2.8	1.8	3.4	6.8	31.3
VENEZUELA	58,747	8.8	6.8	13.4	23.6	4.8	2.9	15.8	6.5	17.4

Country	Total Workers	Professional %	Managerial %	Clerical %	Farming %	Production %	Service %
ARGENTINA	9,011,450	7.5	1.5	23.3	14.4	40.7	12.6
BRAZIL	29,557,224	4.8	2.7	12.7	44.2	25.2	10.4
CHILE	2,607,360	7.1	1.9	17.7	21.1	40.6	11.6
COLOMBIA	5,134,125	3.9	2.6	10.2	47.4	24.7	11.2
ECUADOR	1,528,500	4.4	1.6	10.2	58.6	17.1	8.1
MEXICO	15,597,360	6.2	2.6	16.2	39.3	22.5	13.2
PARAGUAY	754,710	4.2	.6	10.2	48.7	26.7	9.6
PERU	3,786,160	7.6	.4	14.4	40.2	29.1	8.3
URUGUAY	1,012,267	5.6	2.3	21.9	17.8	38.6	13.8
VENEZUELA	3,014,674	7.8	2.5	18.3	20.3	39.1	12.0

Higher Education by Areas of Study

Literacy Rate by Percentage of Population

0%–50%
50%–70%
70%–90%
90%–100%

Workers by Occupation

Adapted from **Statistical Abstract of Latin America:** Vol. 17 (1976), p. 118; Vol. 18 (1977), pp. 143, 192.

According to the map, which countries have the largest number of people who can read and write? Which countries have the smallest number?

What types of jobs do the people in these countries have? What relationship do you see between the literacy rates and the types of jobs found in each country?

How might you explain the college students' choice of studies? Where do you think they are found in the occupation chart? What does their position tell you about the number of college students compared to the total number of working people?

Make some generalizations about the role of education in the development of Latin America. Do the figures lead you to believe that this role may change in years to come? Explain.

Based on the information in the chapter, what changes would you make in the educational system?

Review

public education
teachers

school curriculum
private schools

vocational education
college education

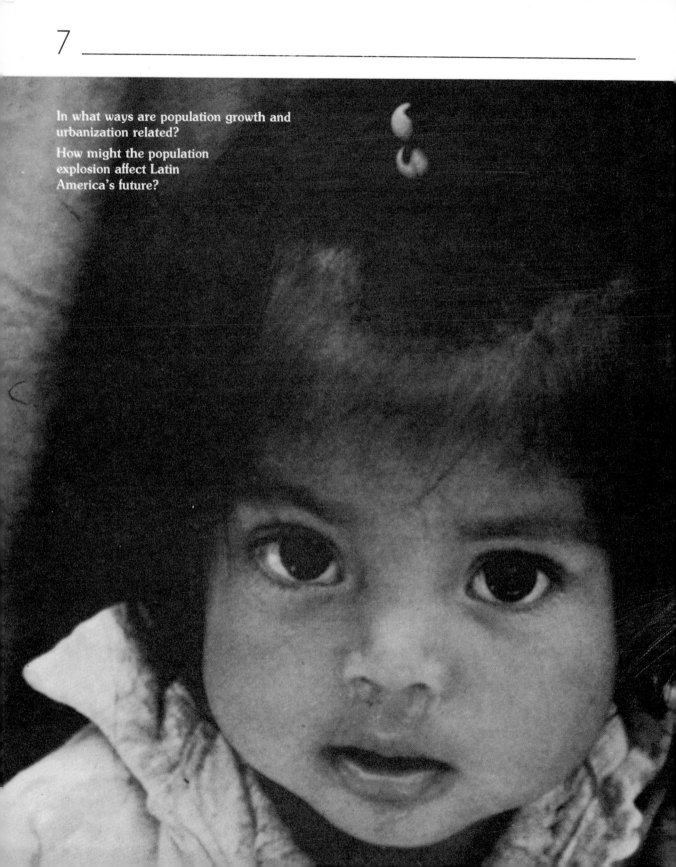

7

In what ways are population growth and urbanization related?

How might the population explosion affect Latin America's future?

Growth and Urbanization

Most visitors to Latin America see only the beauty of the landscape and the warmth of the people. When they visit the cities, they see the shops, the museums, the fancy hotels, and the excitement. What they do not see are the poor areas that plague all major Latin American cities. In Rio de Janeiro and São Paulo, Brazil, these areas are called *favelas*. In Argentina, they are *villas miserias*. In Carácas, Venezuela, the name is *ranchos*, and in Bogotá, Colombia, it is the *tugurios*. The name changes from place to place, but the conditions do not. One author describes these areas in the following way.

> . . . take a journey to misery in Latin America, instead of making the usual enchanting trip to the romance of the sunsets, the beaches, the luxury hotels, and the mansions of those who today are the mighty and the wealthy. . . .
>
> Start with the cities. It does not matter which one. It can be Rio de Janeiro for a start. Climb the nearest hill . . . and you are in the world of the *favela*. It is an ugly world of dirt, piles of garbage, waterless shacks with packing-case walls and corrugated-iron roofs, filthy and sick children playing in refuse, abandoned young mothers, and boys who become *malandros* [street fighters or thieves] before they mature to manhood. . . .
>
> The Rio hills have names that almost tell their own stories; the Hill of the Pig, the Hill of the Dog, the Hill of the Skeleton. . . .
>
> . . . So, etched against the Rio Bay or the blue South Atlantic—one of the world's most beautiful sights—the *favela* stands fermenting in the hot sun, . . . topped by a forest of TV antennas.

From *The Winds of Revolution: Latin America Today—And Tomorrow,* pp. 49–50, by Tad Szulc. Copyright © 1963 by Frederick A. Praeger, Inc. Reprinted by permission of Holt, Rinehart and Winston.

Some people think that the population explosion is bringing the world to the point where there are too many people in it. They say that there are too many to be properly fed, clothed, schooled, housed, and given medical services. This rapid growth of the number of people is one of the factors that has contributed to the slums of Latin America. The problem is made worse by the never-ending flow of people from the countryside to the cities.

Until a short time ago, population growth was thought to be an important part of a country's economic and political strength. More people often meant more workers to help raise the standard of living. It also meant more prestige for the country. But today, hunger and poverty are becoming problems in some areas. Latin America is one of these. Some people have begun to question the wisdom of such rapid population growth. The growth varies from country to country throughout the world. In Europe, for example, the number of people will double in about seventy-five years. In Latin America, it will double in only twenty-five. For these reasons, many people believe that the situation in Latin America will not get better until the birthrate decreases.

Why are some people beginning to question the growing birthrate in Latin America?

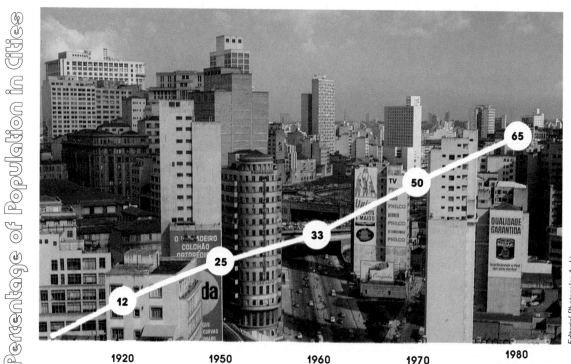

Percentage of Population in Cities

12 — 1920
25 — 1950
33 — 1960
50 — 1970
65 — 1980 Estimate

Editorial Photocolor Archives

The People Explosion—Why? . . .

For many years, Latin America had both a high birthrate and a high death rate. These high birth and death rates offset each other. But, by the 1900's, the death rate was not as high because more Latin Americans began to live longer. One reason for this was immunization against certain diseases. Another was improved sanitary conditions. As a result, most Latin Americans can expect to live at least sixty years.

While the death rate has been decreasing, the birthrate has not. One reason is that until very recently most Latin Americans, especially those of the lower-income group, did not believe in birth control. Those who have come to believe in it give reasons such as the one given by a twenty-nine-year-old Mexican woman who has five children.

> I came to the [family planning] clinic because since I am not able to support them, I no longer want to have more children. I now have five, why more when with these I already have too many? Two or three would be enough. I know that the Church says we should not try to avoid having children, but I believe that it is a greater sin to have them and not educate them. The point is not only to bring them into the world but to educate them also. I am not in accord with those families who have ten or twelve children but can only half dress and feed them, turning them into beggars and delinquents.

Several factors influence the attitudes of most Latin Americans about family planning. One is the stand taken by the Catholic Church. In Latin America, the Church is not in favor of most birth control techniques. Another factor is tradition. It has long been the belief of many Latin American men that one way to demonstrate their *machismo* is to father a lot of children. Still another factor is the lack in some areas of information on family planning. Some experts say that unless things change, the population will keep on growing at a rapid rate. Others say that this is not so. They believe that as Latin America becomes more urban and industrialized, the birthrate will slow down. They predict that this will happen in Latin America by the end of this century.

Why has the death rate decreased in Latin America in recent years? What effect has this had on the population growth of Latin American nations?

For what reasons do some Latin Americans oppose family planning? For what reasons are some in favor of it?

In your opinion, why would industrialization and urbanization influence the birthrate?

Dr. J. Mayone Stycos, "Birth Control," article in *Integration of Man and Society in Latin America* (p. 18), edited by Samuel Shapiro, Copyright © 1967, University of Notre Dame Press.

The Road Goes Only One Way . . . It is the view of some that even with the recent spurt of growth, Latin America is not overpopulated. They say that, although there are a lot of people, there is enough room for all of them. There is a lot of land in Latin America, but much of it is jungle, mountain, or desert. Not many people have settled in these regions. Most Latin Americans live in the coastal regions. Millions live in rural areas and are engaged in farming. These are the people most on the move. Each year, by the thousands, they move to the cities looking for a better education, higher-paying jobs, broader markets, and decent medical care. Most do not find what they seek.

This one-way migration to the cities has caused an uneven distribution of people in Latin America. It has led to overpopulation in the urban areas. Until rural living conditions are improved, such migration is likely to continue. This is true despite the fact that very few migrants find the city a pleasant place to be. Most of them cannot read or write. Most do not have the skills needed for the types of work to be found in the city. As a result, the migrants usually end up in poverty again. Instead of living in a hut in the country, they live in a shantytown at the outskirts of a city or in an area of old, run-down houses. Life in such areas can be hard and in many cases follows the pattern described below.

In such a setting, there is little feeling of community. True, when outside authorities seek to exert control . . . residents may come together in common defense. But . . . they are tied only by the bond of misery, and do not help each other.

Violence is common. A weekend seldom passes without some explosive episode. The men, whose chief recreation is playing a rustic pitch-and-toss game called *tejo* and drinking beer, may dispute a point and fall into a drunken fight with fists or knives. A backyard rivalry . . . among women may result in a stabbing. [Men punish] both their women and their children by beating them, and a mother's [scolding] to a child is often a hard slap or a switch across the face or bottom. Brutality is a part of life, and is accepted.

Unemployment is another fact of life. . . .

. . . Mothers and children are often seen in better neighborhoods begging. Idleness, extreme poverty and need have forced some of the men to become petty sneak thieves; some of the women have turned to prostitution; many of the children have become street gamins [tramps].

Terry L. McCoy,
University of Florida

Sam Schulman, "Latin-American Shantytown," *The New York Times Magazine* (January 16, 1966), p. 33. © 1966/68 by The New York Times Company. Reprinted by permission.

There are, however, positive aspects to the shantytowns. For all their problems, they provide the poor with free or inexpensive housing. Since they pay little or no rent, some shantytown dwellers use their savings to improve their houses and to buy some of the other things they need. These people also tend to want their children to be educated. Many have become interested in law and order. While they do not have a lot of money, most of these people have more than they ever had before. This can be seen in the following story about Blas and Carmen, a young Peruvian couple.

> . . . they rented a two-room, one-storey adobe house in a large lot. . . . The lot was packed solidly with similar houses and the walks between them were about five feet wide. They had filthy, constantly clogged common baths and water taps for every ten houses and the rent was high. They paid extra for electricity and for practically non-existent city services. . . .
>
> [Carmen] did not have too much to do with her neighbors. . . . She found herself being drawn into arguments over petty complaints about children trespassing, dogs barking and messing on the sidewalk, husband's relative success or failure, . . . etc. She was mainly occupied with her son and her new baby daughter, and the constant arguing annoyed Blas more than it did Carmen. Blas had also been disturbed by the crowded conditions. . . .
>
> He had been thinking of moving and . . . Carmen . . . was interested as well. . . . When their landlord told them that he was planning to clear the lot and build a cinema within six months, they decided to move. A colleague of Blas' in the restaurant had spoken to him about a group to which he belonged. The members were organizing an invasion of state land to build houses and they wanted fifty families. . . .
>
> . . . Each family bought its own straw mats and poles for the house, and small groups made arrangements for trucks and taxis. . . . The members had discussed previously what lots they would take, and how the streets were to be laid out and there was very little squabbling during the first day. By early morning when the police arrived there were at least thirty one-room straw houses flying Peruvian flags and the principal streets were outlined with stones.
>
> The police told them they would have to leave. . . . They were told to leave several times but no-one forced them. . . .
>
> Blas and Carmen picked a lot about fifteen by thirty meters on the gradual slope of the hill on the principal street. . . .
>
> Blas and some friends quickly expanded the simple invasion one-room house to a three-room straw mat house and they outlined the lot with stones. He worked hard on Sundays and some nights,

William Mangin, "Urbanization: Case Study in Peru," *Architectural Design*, August 1963, pp. 367–370.

sometimes alone, sometimes with friends. . . . He soon managed to get a brick wall six-and-a-half feet high around his property.

. . . After about a year of working on the lot and making his "plan," Blas decided to contract a "specialist" to help him put up walls for four rooms. He paid for the materials brought by the "specialist" and helped out on the job. When the walls were done he roofed the rooms with cane, bricked up the windows and put in cement floors. With his first pay check, after finishing paying for the walls, Blas made a down payment on a large, elaborate cedar door. . . .

Their principal room fronts on the street and doubles as a shop which Carmen and the oldest children tend. Blas is still a waiter and they now have five children. The saving on rent and the income from the shop make them considerably more prosperous than before. . . .

. . . They own a house which is adequate, Blas has steady work, their oldest children are in school, and Blas has been on the elected committee that runs barriada [shantytown] affairs and feels that he has some say in local government. . . .

. . . They feel, in comparison to people like themselves and in terms of their own aspirations, that they have done well. When asked what they would do if they acquired a large sum of money, they both answer in terms of improving their present property and educating their children.

Why do so many Latin Americans migrate from the country to the city? What problems do these migrants encounter in the city? In your opinion, why do they stay in the city instead of returning home?

What kind of living conditions do most migrants encounter? Do you think Blas and Carmen's story is a typical one? Why or why not? What does their "success" suggest about Latin America's future urban development?

The Other Side of the Story . . . Almost all migrants, whether they do well or not, tend to stay in the city. For this reason, urban populations have soared. This has made heavy demands on the people and the government. Jobs and housing must be found for these people. They must have health services. There must be an on-going expansion of such public services as education, welfare, street and sidewalk care, and water, light, and sewage systems. For the most part, these services are ample only in the central part of the cities where the better housing areas are found.

In the last few years, more and more attractive suburbs have begun to spring up just outside the cities. These new areas are drawing middle-income and wealthy people. Then, too, some countries like Mexico have begun to carry out programs of urban renewal. Some of these have had amazing results. They have replaced slums with low-income housing.

Robert Hatton

Latin American cities have grown rapidly in the last twenty-five years. Bogotá, Colombia, shown here, is one of several cities whose population more than doubled during this time.

And the cities, even with their problems, offer variety and excitement to many. As shown in the following reading, for many the city life is the better life.

As I sat down on his folding chair, Juan Rodríguez Lozano, the bootblack who kept station on the sidewalk outside my hotel, handed me the morning's edition of *Novedades*. I had scarcely glanced at the headlines when Juan interrupted his rhythmic brushing to pull a wristwatch from his shirt pocket. I could have it for 200 little pesos, he said. . . .

"But Juan," I said, "I already have a watch."

"Yesterday I had a customer who offered to buy it, but he had no money and wanted to owe me. You who can afford it don't need the watch. *Así es la vida*—that's life. As I told you the other day, I have just finished making payments on my little house. Now I need money to pay the lawyer for the paper work."

With pride in his voice Juan had told me of his house. Buying it had been a major event in his life, a turning point. Before, Juan and his wife and twin sons had lived in a city slum, and before that in a poor village.

It was a hard life, shining shoes, but Juan was making progress. And he was doing it in the great city of Mexico.

Exciting and interesting things were always happening here. Juan was in the thick of them, his work station . . . situated near one of the main downtown intersections. . . .

On the sidewalks eddied crowds of people who come from every part of the Mexican nation—and indeed, of the world. Within range of our eyes some of the most modern, most [boldly] designed buildings to be found anywhere soared over Spanish-colonial masterpieces of outstanding beauty. The very atmosphere pulsated with the hustle and bustle of a people on the go.

What are some of the ways rapid urban population growth can affect a country?

What do you think are some of the benefits of living in a city like Mexico City?

Louis de la Haba, "Mexico, the City That Founded a Nation," *National Geographic*, Vol. 143, No. 5 (May 1973), p. 641.

_____

A New Way of Life . . . The following is the story of one Peruvian family who left their home in the country to move to the city.

Don Valentín Punarejo was a *serrano* [a person from the mountain regions] . . . in Puno, a department and town in southern Peru. . . . He was forty-six years old, married to Doña Lorenza Rodríguez de Punarejo, and the father of two daughters, Susana, eleven years old, and Consuelo, two. He owned land, a house . . . , and a herd of twenty cattle. . . . he would buy cattle from his neighbors and acquaintances in Puno, giving them only a first payment down and paying the rest after he had sold the cattle. He would drive the cattle to Lima in fifteen or sixteen days and sell them there at the slaughterhouse of the Terminal [the Wholesale and Retail Market of Lima]. . . .

Perhaps he convinced himself of the city's advantages; at any rate he decided that since he spent so much time in Lima it would be better to move his family there. . . .

With the family somewhat settled [about a month later], Don Valentín went back to Puno to buy cattle. There he discovered that his old friends and associates would no longer accept just part-payment for their animals. . . .

Doña Lorenza suffered in the new surroundings—from the "heat" of Lima, . . . from separation from her family and friends and the animals she had cared for in her old home, and even from the frustration of radio programs in a language which she could not understand. Susana, on the contrary, enjoyed her new life. She no longer had to carry water in buckets from the well, . . . and she did not have to take the sheep out to pasture. The [new] house . . . had a kerosene stove, electric lights, and running water. . . . She enjoyed going . . . to the movies, and to the street carnivals. She was even more enthusiastic about her enrollment in school. . . .

. . . In the hope of holding on to some of his capital, Don Valentín bought a retail stall in the Terminal. Contrary to the word of the previous owner, the stall had practically no business. . . . He attempted to sell his unprofitable stall but was offered only half the price he paid for it. A trip to Puno to retain his house and land ended unsuccessfully in a forced sale.

In the midst of these economic troubles, a son was born. To cut expenses, the family moved into a single room in the Terminal itself. Later another son was born. . . . Doña Lorenza began serving meals to people at the Terminal, earning most of the family's income. . . .

Don Valentín is now fifty-eight years old and looks much older. He has not perfected his Spanish. . . . He no longer wears boots or even shoes, having gone back to the cheap sandals made from truck tires. . . . his main pleasure is to drink with a friend. His clothes are no longer kept clean. He makes no attempt to attract customers to his fruit cart. . . .

Richard Patch, "La Parada, Lima Market: Part I: A Villager Who Met Disaster," *American Universities Field Staff Report,* (West Coast South American Series, Vol. XIV, No. 1: Hanover, New Hampshire, 1967), pp. 4–7, 10.

Explain how the family members have had to change to fit into their new way of life. What has living in the city done to the relationships among the family members?

Who do you think benefited from the move to the city? Who suffered?

Where would you place the responsibility for some of the family's problems? Why do you think this family's experience turned out so differently from that of Blas and Carmen?

EXPLORATION

Estimates of the Population of Latin America and the World, 1650–1975

Date	Latin America (millions)	World (millions)	Latin America (percent of world)
1650	12	545	2.2
1750	16	791	2.0
1850	38	1262	3.0
1900	74	1650	4.5
1950	163	2517	6.5
1960	213	3005	7.1
1970	277	3632	7.6
1975	319	4014	7.9

Barry Edmonston, "Latin American population—a changing phenomenon," *Latin American Digest,* Vol. 10, No. 2 (Late Winter 1976), p. 1.

Discuss the population growth in Latin America in the last 300 years. Based on the information in the chart, has the growth in Latin America been steady from century to century? From decade to decade? Explain.

How does the population growth in this century compare with that of earlier centuries? How does Latin American population growth compare with the world population growth?

What effect do you think such growth has had on past development in Latin America? What influence do you think it will have in the future?

Some say that slowing down population growth is not the answer to Latin America's urban problems. They feel that a society must produce or it will have a low standard of living no matter what the number of people is. They feel that it would help if each person would produce more. This could create the wealth and new ideas needed to solve the problems. These experts say that it is more important, therefore, to focus on greater productivity than to attack population growth. Based on the information in this chapter, do you think that the experts are right or wrong? Explain.

Review

population explosion
family planning

country-to-city migration
shantytowns

urban development
city life

8

What is the role of the *campesino* and of agriculture in Latin America?

Why is agrarian reform needed in Latin America?

The Land of the Campesino

From Christmas until early summer the cane is cut, and much cane is planted. The fields are alive with activity. Long lines of men stand before the cane like soldiers before an enemy. The machetes [heavy knives] sweep down and across the stalks, cutting them close to the ground. The leaves are lopped off, the stalk cut in halves or thirds and dropped behind. It is a beautiful thing to watch from a hundred yards' distance. The men seem tiny but implacable, moving steadily against a green forest which recedes before them. When the cane has been piled and then scooped up, . . . the oxen may graze among the trash. . . .

From a distance, the scene is toylike and wholesome. Up close it is neither. The men sweat freely; the cane chokes off the breeze, and the pace of cutting is awesome. The men's shirts hang loose and drip sweat continuously. The hair of the cane pierces the skin and works its way down the neck. The ground is furrowed and makes footing difficult, and the soil gives off heat like an oven. The mayordomo [overseer] sits astride a roan mare and supervises the field operations. He wears khakis and cordovan riding accessories. To see him ride past a line of men bent over and dripping sweat, to hear the sounds of the oxen in the fields behind, the human and animal grunting, and to feel the waves of heat billowing out of the ground and cane evoke images of other times. The men of Jauca grow drawn in the first two weeks of the harvest. This is the time to make the money to pay debts from the past dead time and to prepare for the next.

In Latin America today, farm workers are learning to expect more out of life than poverty. In the past, the *campesinos,* the people who live and work in the country, visited mainly the villages nearest them. Today, improved roads and bus service bring these people into the large urban areas. These trips to the city along with radios, movies, and television have given the peasants a glimpse of a better life. But the *campesinos* have yet to gain a higher standard of living. And this has led to frustration. As a result, in some Latin American countries, the farm workers have taken part in strikes and have taken over large estates. They want agrarian reforms, which means great changes in the social, economic, and political structure of rural areas.

Sidney W. Mintz, *Worker in the Cane,* pp. 20–21. © 1960 by Yale University Press. Reprinted by permission of Yale University Press.

Latin American farmers make up about 50 percent of the population. Still, they are failing to feed their people; many Latin Americans still do not get enough to eat. Farm products are needed in Latin America not only to feed the people but also to bring in earnings through exports. These earnings are used to pay for imported food and industrial goods. But expansion of farm exports has been slow while the need for imported goods has been rising rapidly. For that reason, most Latin American countries suffer from a continuing balance-of-trade deficit. This means that they are paying more for their imports than they are earning for their exports.

Why does Latin America need more farm output?

Most Latin American farmers work other people's land in exchange for a share of the crops. These Mexican farmers are planting corn with digging sticks.

Peter Arnold, Inc. by Jacques Jangoux

The ranching and cattle industry was introduced in Latin America by the Spanish colonists. The *hacienda* system still controls most of the land. This worker is driving cattle on a Mexican *hacienda*.

The *Hacienda* . . . In most Latin American countries, only a few people own almost all the land. In fact, some 10 percent own 90 percent of it. Large ranches called *haciendas* account for the greater part of the big landholdings. Most of the work on these ranches is done by peasant sharecroppers. The *hacendado,* or owner, rules over the peasants and tells them when and what to plant. In most cases, each worker keeps one third or one half of the crop and gives the rest to the *hacendado.* The peasants must work in the fields and provide other services, such as repairing fences. On some *haciendas,* sharecroppers earn a small wage. The *hacendado* gives them a hut, a small piece of land, seeds, simple tools, and at times, work animals. Since a store and religious and social activities also are provided, there is little need to leave the grounds. This social and economic power allows the *hacendado* to dominate the local area.

The sharecropping system gives the *hacendados* a lot of cheap labor. They have no real need for up-to-date farm machinery or training. Most work is done by hand, and the amount produced per acre is quite low. Much of the land is not farmed at all. Most *hacendados* plant only about 10 to 15 percent of their land at one time. Taxes on these lands are low. Therefore, the *hacendado* feels no push to produce more or to sell the land to a bold tenant farmer who wants to buy it.

Through its influence on the peasants, the *hacienda* system holds back economic progress in still another way. Because they get little or nothing for all their work, most peasants do not have enough money to buy many manufactured goods. This means that there is a lack of consumers. This lack, in turn, stops new industry from growing. That means no new jobs. The system also discourages the peasants from trying to improve their lot. The story of Fabiano is an example of this.

In the division of stock at the year's end, Fabiano received a fourth of the calves and a third of the kids, but as he grew no feed, . . . he disposed of the animals. . . .

If he could only put something aside for a few months, he would be able to get his head up. Oh, he had made plans, but that was all foolishness. . . . Once the beans had been eaten and the ears of corn gnawed, there was no place to go but to the boss's cash drawer. He would turn over the animals that had fallen to his lot for the lowest of prices, grumbling and protesting in distress. . . . Arguing, he would choke and bite his tongue. Dealing with anyone else he would not let himself be so shamelessly robbed, but, as he was afraid of being put off the ranch, he would give in. He would take the cash and listen to the advice that accompanied it. . . . He would stand there with his mouth open, red-faced, his throat swelling. . . .

Little by little the boss's brand was put on Fabiano's stock, and when he had nothing left to sell, [he] went into debt. . . .

This time, as on other occasions, Fabiano first made a deal regarding the stock, then thought better of the matter. . . . he went to consult with his wife. Vitória sent the boys to play in the clay pit, sat down in the kitchen, and concentrated, lining up different kinds of seeds on the ground, adding and subtracting. The next day Fabiano went back to town, but on closing the deal he noted that, as usual, Vitória's figuring differed from that of the boss. He protested, and received the usual explanation: the difference represented interest.

He refused to accept this answer. . . . Surely there was some mistake on the boss's paper. The mistake couldn't be found, and Fabiano lost his temper. . . .

The boss became angry. He refused to hear such insolence. He thought it would be a good thing if the herdsman looked for another job.

At this point Fabiano got cold feet and began to back down. . . . His wife must just be mistaken, that was all. . . .

The boss calmed down and Fabiano backed out of the room, his hat dragging on the brick floor. . . .

He looked at the bills neatly flattened out in his hand and at the silver and nickel coins; he sighed and bit his lips. He didn't even have the right to protest. He had drawn in his horns, for if he had not he would have had to leave the ranch and take to the road with his wife, his small sons, and his scanty belongings. And where would they go?

Graciliano Ramos, *Barren Lives,* trans. Ralph Edward Dimmick (Austin: University of Texas Press, 1965), pp. 93–97. Copyright © 1965 by Heloisa de Medeiros Ramos. All rights reserved.

Peasants continue to work on the *hacienda* for several reasons. In some cases, they are held there by tradition. To leave would be to desert the same land their ancestors had tilled. In other cases, they are chained by the debts they owe the *hacendado*. For those who are free from debt and want to leave, there are few choices. They cannot expect to acquire their own land. Moving to another *hacienda* will not improve their lives. Their only hope for a better life lies in the city, but that means adapting to urban life.

How does the *hacienda* system work? Why is the *hacendado* so powerful?

In what ways does the *hacienda* system hold back Latin American progress?

Why do the peasants continue to work on the *haciendas*?

If you were a peasant, how would you feel about the *hacienda* system and the power of the *hacendado*?

Produce comes to town from the commercial farm by the truckload. Since refrigeration is not common, it must quickly be unloaded and prepared for sale.

The Commercial Farm and Other Landholdings . . .

Not all of the large landholdings in Latin America are *haciendas*. Some are commercial farms which produce bananas, sugar, coffee, meat, cereals, and wool for sale on the world market. On these farms all is done to be efficient. A great deal of money is spent on the machines, fertilizers, and insecticides that will help the farmers use their land to the fullest. Workers are given certain tasks, and they work set hours. In return, they receive fairly good, fixed wages. They also may receive medical and educational services. Still, most of them work only during the four-month harvest season. Commercial farms are important to the Latin American economy. Their products are needed for both export and home use. These farms produce more than half of the export earnings of Argentina, Brazil, Colombia, the Dominican Republic, Ecuador, Guatemala, Honduras, Nicaragua, and Uruguay.

Latin American farms may range in size from hundreds of thousands of acres to less than an acre. This Indian family in Guatemala hopes to produce enough to eat from this small plot of land.

Steven A. Seidman

Not all landholdings in Latin America are large. One kind of small farm is the Mexican *ejido,* which is owned by a community of people. There are two kinds of *ejidos.* One is the individual *ejido,* which is a piece of land the community gives a person for personal use. The land cannot be sold or mortgaged. It must be cultivated for two years, or it will be turned over to someone else. The other is the collective *ejido,* a farm on which the members work together. Each member's share of the harvest depends on how much labor the member has contributed.

The most common type of small farms are the *minifundias,* two to fifteen acre farms found throughout Latin America. For the most part, the farms are too small and the soil is too poor to provide a decent living for the family that owns or works them. The Santos family of Guatemala, discussed below, is typical of many of the small farmers in Latin America.

> [The] hillside near San Antonio shows many characteristics of highland farming. The fields are small, as well as steep, since they have been passed down from generation to generation, divided among brothers and sisters for hundreds of years. . . . Since the highland farmer knows little about the use of fertilizer, and has scant extra cash with which to buy it anyway, the nutriments in the thin soil are used up in several years. . . .
>
> Men are clearing the ground on both sides of the fallow field for new planting. The work they can do is limited entirely by the strength of their bodies, and the skill with which they use two simple tools: the *machete,* a big wide-bladed knife, and the *azadón,* a long-handled heavy hoe. They have no machinery, not even oxen or burros, to help them cultivate the land or carry their crops home. . . .

Field workers grind corn into silage for cattle feed. Shown here is *Ejido Ixtapaluca,* a communal farm formed under Mexico's land reform program.

Maíz [corn] has been planted in other fields on this hillside. Here Emilio Santos . . . hoes his land, chopping out weeds, working his way carefully around the peanut vines he has planted in between the *maíz*. . . .

Emilio Santos is one of the oldest men in San Antonio. He has been working his land in the same way for more than fifty years. He was taught to farm by his father and grandfather. He learned when he was very young to use religious signs to decide on the best days to plant, and then to weed carefully around the tender young corn. He learned to pick a few ears after four months to eat fresh and to harvest the rest a month later, when the corn is dry and suitable for grinding into meal.

When Emilio's crops are good, he gives thanks to the Christian god and to his favorite saints, just as his Mayan ancestors made offerings to their gods. When his crops are damaged by erosion, storm, insects, or plant diseases, there is little he can do to save them.

The Guatemalan government has a pilot project in San Antonio to encourage people to use modern farming practices. . . .

For a number of reasons, San Antonio farmers are slow to accept these ideas. . . . Their lives and the lives of their families depend completely upon the success of their crops, and since they can barely support themselves now, they dare not take risks. In addition, most farmers have so little extra cash that they must feel convinced the crops will show a marked improvement before they will lay out money for treated seeds, insecticides, and fertilizers.

How does the commercial farm compare with the *hacienda*?

How do commercial farms affect the Latin American economy?

What is a *minifundia*? An *ejido*? Why are these smaller farms important?

What do you think can be done to improve the lot of small farmers like Emilio Santos?

Agrarian Reform . . . Most Latin American peasants want agrarian reforms. The experts have different ideas on how to bring about the needed changes. They are:

(1) Raise the land taxes to force the big ranch owners to plant or sell more land.

(2) Colonize, settle, and develop frontier lands.

(3) Make laws to guarantee working conditions and a minimum wage for farm workers.

(4) Urge the peasants to engage in commercial farming.

(5) Set up group farms for small farmers.

(6) Bring in more industry to create more jobs.

(7) Break up the large estates, and divide the land among the peasants.

David Mangurian

Land reform programs have followed many different patterns in the various Latin American countries. Above: A sign at a bus stop on Peru's *altiplano* suggests that agrarian reform is still a live issue. Right: The International Potato Center in Lima, Peru, tries to develop better varieties of potatoes. Here, workers weigh a new kind of potato.

David Mangurian

A young farmer in Paraguay clears the jungle land around his home. He then will use the land to plant crops.

David Mangurian

The following reading tells what happened in Bolivia when several of the ideas were tried.

Nearly three-quarters of all Bolivians are farmers, among the most poverty-stricken in Latin America. Since the cultivated part of Bolivia is only a small part of the whole, colonization has seemed the best solution. But the projects to accomplish it are running into trouble. Some of the colonists drift back home. Others go back to the old ways of farming rather than try to work with new machines and red tape.

Individual pioneering is doing better. Often all that is needed is a road of sorts. In the old days, landowners often held several haciendas. During the dry season on the plateau, they would send their people down to cultivate damper, warmer fields, bringing them back when the rains started on the heights. Some Indians are now following this pattern on their own. After a few years they no longer come back; sometimes they push on fur-

ther down, hacking out new fields, leaving the old for less bold newcomers.

Another example of colonization can be found in the remote Chapare area of Cochabamba. There employees of an oil company that stopped working stayed on to farm. This spark of enterprise among a people cowed for centuries and supposedly bound by tradition is one of the unexpected results of such reform.

Another is their entrance into the market economy. They have been quick to discover crops that pay. They are also learning to rent a truck and carry their produce right to market, avoiding the middlemen. Some have moved into town and become merchants themselves.

Adapted from Gladys Delmas, "Bolivia: Revolution in Mid-Passage," *The Reporter*, December 1, 1966, pp. 31–34.

What kinds of agrarian reform were used in Bolivia?

What were the benefits of these reforms? What were the drawbacks?

Why do you think some people say that the social benefits are greater and more important than the economic ones?

What effect, if any, have these reforms had on the peasants? On farm production? On the economy?

What agrarian reforms do you feel would be of the most worth? The least worth? Explain.

| COUNTRY | AVERAGE SUPPLY OF PROTEINS | | | | AVERAGE CALORIES CONSUMED IN RELATION TO NEEDS (%) | | |
| | POP. IN 1,000'S | | GRAMS PER DAY | | | | |
	1961	1970	1961	1970	1961	1970	1973
ARGENTINA	21,203	24,304	97.7	98.6	116.5	123.9	122.9
BOLIVIA	3,778	4,658	43.2	45.8	68.7	80.8	89.7
BRAZIL	71,845	93,029	60.7	63.3	103.3	109.4	119.7
CHILE	7,882	9,780	66.8	70.9	97.8	114.6	109.3
COLOMBIA	15,878	21,363	49.8	50.8	94.4	96.6	92.3
EDUADOR	4,498	6,089	46.2	49.0	82.4	88.9	79.1
GUATEMALA	580	5,111	53.4	58.7	82.2	93.3	98.1
PARAGUAY	1,785	2,406	76.1	73.5	112.2	122.9	106.1
PERU	10,323	13,587	61.0	61.5	98.1	98.7	102.5
URUGUAY	2,575	2,886	110.2	95.6	116.3	113.1	128.5
VENEZUELA	8,004	10,755	58.6	62.3	91.6	101.7	98.8

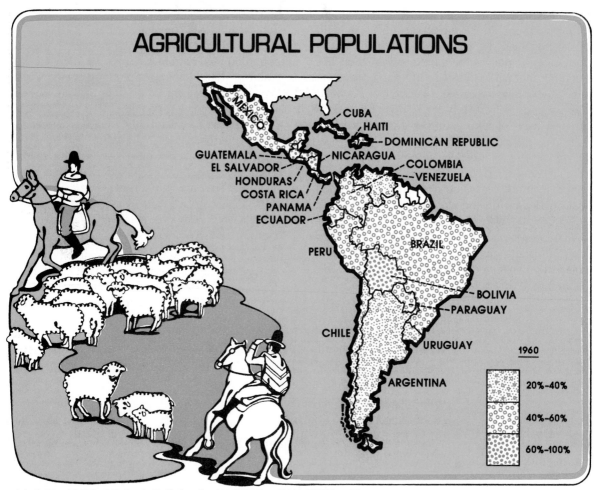

AGRICULTURAL POPULATIONS

1960

20%–40%

40%–60%

60%–100%

Adapted from **Statistical Abstract of Latin America:** Vol. 17 (1976), p. 51; Vol. 18 (1977), p. 34.

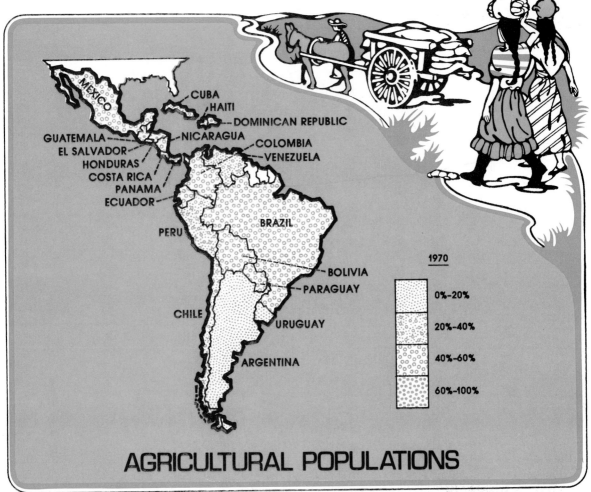

AGRICULTURAL POPULATIONS

1970

- 0%-20%
- 20%-40%
- 40%-60%
- 60%-100%

Adapted from **Statistical Abstract of Latin America:** Vol. 17 (1976), p. 51; Vol. 18 (1977), p. 34.

Which countries probably have the best-fed people? The worst-fed? On what did you base your answers?

Using the maps, tell which countries had the largest percentage of farmers in 1970. Which had the smallest? What is the relationship between the percentage of a country's farm labor force and the kind of diet it has?

The maps show fewer people in farming in 1970 than in 1960. Based on this and on the information found in Chapters 7 and 8, why do you think this is happening?

Based on the information in the maps, charts, and chapters, do you think there is a need for agrarian reform? Explain your answer.

Review

campesino
hacienda system
power of the hacendado

commercial farm
ejido

minifundia
agrarian reform

9

What were the characteristics of traditional Latin American politics?

What was the role of the military and the *caudillo* in Latin American politics?

A Political Tradition

Melgarejo, the soldier who had so boldly taken the leading role in the overthrow of the president was a man without the most basic notion of the ways of government. He did not even represent any political belief. He was not supported by anyone who, on his own, could have raised a banner that would have captured the sympathies of the masses. For the moment there was only one sure fact. Melgarejo had engineered a revolution. But for whom?

A man of humblest origin, his education was the training he had in the barracks. Melgarejo's whole life was made up of treason and crimes.

Before it had been in power a month, the new government issued two decrees. By a stroke of the pen, they did away with the Constitution of 1861.

The country began to show alarm. It plainly saw that this soldier would trample underfoot all its institutions. Armed protests broke out, in the name of upholding the Constitution.

After Melgarejo put down the revolts, the whole country gave up. And the same men who in secret talked against using force yielded too and forsook their principles. They even went further. Many rushed to offer their services to the victor, who found himself surrounded, through fear, by the best elements in the country.

At this time, it was very fashionable to drink many toasts at the palace banquets. Each of the guests was eager to show his allegiance.

When his turn came, one of the guests spoke in words of praise of the new charter which would surely govern the acts of Melgarejo.

Melgarejo's instant response was brutal.

"I want the gentleman who has just spoken and all the deputies gathered here to know that I have put the Constitution of 1861, which was very good, in this pocket" (pointing to his left trouser pocket) "and that of 1868, which is even better in the opinion of these gentlemen, in this one" (pointing to his right pocket). "Nobody is going to rule in Bolivia but me."

In the 1800's, men like Melgarejo ruled Latin American politics. Now the main themes in Latin American politics are social reforms and the building of democratic governments. More and more of the Latin American people are taking part in what is done in their countries. In Melgarejo's time, this was not true. Then there were only a few who spoke up for the poor.

Adapted from Alcides Arguedas, "Los caudillos bárbaros," *The Green Continent,* ed. Germán Arciniegas, trans. Harriet De Onís (New York: Alfred A. Knopf, Inc., 1944), pp. 205–207, 222.

BACKGROUND

In the 1800's, political affairs in Latin America were under the control of a small but strong group of people. This group was made up of rich landowners, army officers, clergy, merchants, intellectuals, and professionals. Most of the rest of the people could not read or write and were powerless. They accepted the rule of the minority. Most Latin Americans either failed to vote or voted as they were ordered by those in power. The situation in Mexico, described below, was not uncommon.

> The respectable Creoles [those of European descent but born in the Americas], as a rule, avoided politics. The type of self-made general with whom they would have to deal filled them with disgust. They were content to live apart while the country was bled by its military parasites. Life in the capital continued to be gay and reckless. There were cockfights and bullfights and the eternal round of flirting and parading on the streets—the games of a class that had no useful thing to do.
>
> There were exceptions among them—men who fought for a new and finer country. But they were too few and far between to change the picture very much. While an unpaid army was fighting to keep Texas in the Republic, there was little to show in the capital that Mexico was facing the gravest crisis in its history.

Adapted from *Many Mexicos*, p. 231, by Lesley Byrd Simpson. © 1952, 1966 by Lesley Byrd Simpson; reprinted by permission of the University of California Press.

The life of the peasant in Latin America always has been a difficult one. A trip to the local market often was the only time spent away from home. This is a scene from the market at Orizaba, Mexico, in the 1800's.

The Bettmann Archive, Inc.

Rich Brommer

Father Miguel Hidalgo y Costilla (1753–1811) is one of Mexico's famous heroes. On September 16, 1810, in the town of Dolores, he made an appeal for troubled peoples. This led to the Mexican Revolution.

For the most part, the few who wanted democracy in Latin America were divided into conservatives and liberals. In most ways, there was very little difference between the two. What differences there were often led to revolutions and civil war. Both wanted to keep most things the way they were. Their main interests were form of government and Church-State relations. The conservatives wanted a strong central government with a powerful president and a weak legislature. The liberals wanted local self-rule and a strong legislature to control the president. Neither group seemed to care much about helping the lower class. The conservative upper class and clergy wanted to keep the social system the same as it had been for years. The liberal merchants and professionals fought for changes that would bring them more wealth, social status, and political power. The liberals wanted to curb the influence of the Church and the army. Their attacks on the Catholic Church met with a fair amount of success. Their attacks on the army did not have much effect.

What groups controlled Latin American politics in the 1800's? Why were these groups so powerful?

What were the differences between the conservatives and the liberals? What did they have in common?

Historical Pictures Service, Inc.

General Antonio Lopéz de Santa Anna (1791–1876) ruled Mexico three times as president but was always overthrown.

Historical Pictures Service, Inc.

General Juan Manuel de Rosas (1793–1877) controlled Argentina for almost twenty-five years. His rule was a time of much cruelty.

The Power of the Strong . . . During the 1800's, most Latin American nations did not have armed forces like the ones they have had in recent years. The soldiers did not have professional training, and most of them were loyal to their leader rather than to their nation. These leaders were known as *caudillos.* The military bands they headed had gained experience and won respect in the early 1800's during the fights for independence.

There was no tradition of civilian control of the army, but political groups often encouraged the soldiers. When a group was out of power and had no hope of winning an election, it could back a *caudillo* who was willing to bring down the government in power. At times, a group in office, afraid of losing the next election, would not submit to the test of the ballot box. In that case, opposing groups could call on a *caudillo* to bring down that

Historical Pictures Service, Inc.

Historical Pictures Service, Inc.

General Porfirio Diaz (1830–1915) was president of Mexico for thirty years. There was progress, but he was criticized for allowing foreign investments.

General Andrés Santa Cruz (1792–1865) ruled Bolivia for ten years. His one great aim was to create a Peru-Bolivian union which never came about.

government. All of these conditions helped bring about a political atmosphere in which the army could step in quite easily. The military leaders had most of the power. They could use this power to force themselves on a country, at least until someone else led another revolt.

Caudillos had charge of many Latin American countries in the 1800's, and, in some cases, in the 1900's. Some ruled the whole country while others controlled only parts of a country. Although most were mestizos, they came from all kinds of backgrounds and ethnic groups. They were very different in personal and political style and in their impact on the countries they ruled. Most of them were in the armed forces. Some, like Santa Anna in Mexico, were regular army officers. Others, such as Facundo in Argentina, raised their own military bands. The few who were not soldiers still needed the support of the army.

Rafael Trujillo, Jr., is shown at a meeting with the press following his father's assassination in May, 1961.

Bob Henriques for Magnum

The power of the *caudillo* did not end with the nineteenth century. A more recent example was Rafael Trujillo, who ruled the Dominican Republic from 1930–1961. Below is one journalist's description and opinion of Trujillo's rule.

> Dominican history came to a head in Trujillo; he was the most typical and most brutal representative of a long tradition. . . . His success was due to his technique of slowly turning the whole country into a private estate of the Trujillo family.
>
> The Trujillo Trust held the monopolies for tobacco, coffee, cocoa, salt, matches, and minerals. The Trujillo clan ran the lottery and the transportation system. The Trujillos were also the largest cattle dealers in the state. They owned the biggest slaughterhouse and set the prices for meat and milk. The president had soldiers run his dairy herds, then sold the milk to the government party. It was paid for by a special tax on government officials. "God and Trujillo give you milk"—this lesson was impressed upon everyone in the Dominican Republic.

Adapted from an Excerpt from *The Red, White, and Black Continent*, pp. 94–95, by Herbert Wendt. Copyright © 1966 by Doubleday & Company, Inc. Used by permission of Doubleday & Company, Inc.

Trujillo was very fond of being compared with God. Every water fountain in the capital, which had been renamed Ciudad Trujillo, bore the inscription "God and Trujillo supply you with water!" Under a shade tree one might see, "You owe this shade to God and Trujillo." On the main streets, neon lights proclaimed "God and Trujillo!" At times Trujillo put himself first. The number plate of every car in the Dominican Republic bore the slogan "Long live Trujillo!" All driver's licenses were adorned with *"Viva Trujillo!"* No newspaper in the Dominican Republic could mention Trujillo's name without also citing his official titles: "President of the Republic, Generalissimo, Benefactor of the Nation, Liberator of the Fatherland, Restorer of Financial Independence, Founder and Supreme Leader of the Dominican Party, Protector of Art and the Sciences."

The "Father of the Fatherland," as he also called himself, was a great invoker of God. He hoped the Vatican would show proper gratitude and at least give him the title of "Benefactor of the Church." But the Vatican was only too well informed on the many executions and poisonings. Rome therefore politely turned him down. He received a similar rejection when he proposed himself for the Nobel Peace Prize. After the end of World War II, Trujillo was urged to allow a political opposition. He did so, in his own way. He set up a few parties whose programs differed in no way from his own and which gave him their votes.

In any case, on May 30, 1961, The Benefactor sank under a hail of bullets from rebel army officers.

How did the military gain so much prestige and power?

How could a *caudillo* become so powerful? How did the political parties help a *caudillo* gain control?

Why do you think the large masses of Latin American people tolerated such leaders as Rafael Trujillo? What do you think led to Trujillo's downfall?

John Littlewood for Black Star

The economy of the Dominican Republic still relies on agriculture. These workers are shown on a state farm during the time of Trujillo.

The Presidency—Two Views . . . Every Latin American nation has had a variety of governments and presidents. Venezuela is no exception. The excerpts which follow describe the politics of two Venezuelan leaders, General José Monagas and Antonio Guzmán Blanco. Each served as president of Venezuela in the 1800's.

Organization of American States

General José Monagas

General José Monagas had come up from the Venezuelan *llanos*. He wore the halo of a patriot and a hero. Monagas became a liberal, turning against those who had first elected him. He had great ambitions of his own and wanted no advice.

First, Monagas strengthened his hold over the army. He ruled the cabinet and chose weak Liberal ministers who let him staff government jobs. The showdown between the two branches of government came soon after: Monagas overpowered congress. Congress tried to impeach him, but it failed. In 1848, he got back by destroying the independence of the legislative body.

Monagas also made good use of Antonio Leocadio Guzmán, whom he named vice-president and minister of the interior. He needed Guzmán to win the support of the press and the people, and thus add to his own power.

As president, Monagas made few changes and no improvements. When, sure of his own great powers, he tried to change the constitution in 1857 so he could succeed himself, he led the way to his own fall. In spite of the wedge he tried to drive between the liberals and conservatives, the issue brought together the two groups enough to bring about his downfall.

Adapted from Harry Bernstein, *Venezuela & Colombia,* © 1946, pp. 42–43. Adapted by permission of Prentice-Hall, Inc., Englewood Cliffs, New Jersey.

Historical Pictures Service, Inc.

Antonio Guzmán Blanco

Old Antonio Leocadio Guzmán, the journalist, politician, and man of the people, had married into the Blanco family, members of the Caracas upper class. In 1828 his son, Antonio Guzmán Blanco, was born.

The Guzmán Blanco era began when young Guzmán Blanco, using his own talents and the influence of his father, joined in with the *caudillos* of the provinces. He organized them and spoke for them.

Antonio Guzmán Blanco brought Venezuela out of civil war into a forced prosperity and a one-*caudillo* rule. Beginning as a liberal, he broke with that party when it seemed to be winning. He launched his new career as the leader of generals, although he was not a soldier. He entered Caracas as a victor in April 1870, at the head of a movement called *Regeneración* (Regeneration). He became president for a first term of almost eight years, from 1870 to 1877. Guzmán Blanco was well aware of Venezuelan problems and needs. And he brought to his task a new, modern approach.

No doubt exists about what was accomplished under his long rule. It was a period of much material development. Venezuela and Venezuelans made money. A good many funds were given over to public works and building railways, piers, and roads. There were a lot of contracts and profits. At the same time, Guzmán Blanco began the effort to start the long road toward education for all. He also created the modern city of Caracas as the center of a network of roads, ports, and telegraphic communications. His major accomplishment, in fact, was in the reform of Venezuela's Church-State relations.

Ibid., pp. 46–47.

Identify and give examples of the differences and similarities between the two views of a president's role.

What methods were used by each of the leaders to gain and keep power? Which leader do you think was more effective? Why and in what ways? How, if at all, did each influence his country? The political process?

Why do you think both of these leaders are described as *caudillos*?

Benito Juárez, the president of Mexico, was a nineteenth-century political leader. His story is as follows:

Benito Juárez . . . was the first Indian ruler since Cuauhtémoc [the last Aztec ruler]. Benito grew up in the lovely southern town of Oaxaca, where he lived in the streets most of the time, more often hungry than not. On Saturdays he wandered through the market, picking up a few centavos, whenever he could, by running errands. . . . Often he sat in the evening, listening quietly to marimba players under the plaza trees or watching men leap and shout in the ancient feather dance of his people. Sometimes he went into the church to stand silently. . . .

As Benito grew older, a priest noticed the thoughtful black eyes under shaggy hair and offered to teach him. The boy learned quickly. He went to school and later studied law. And then, while still a young man, he became Governor of Oaxaca.

Benito Juárez was a good governor. People talked of him with respect because he was honest, and he saw that those who worked under him were honest. Where so many officials accepted bribes and made fortunes one way or another while in office, Juárez was never known to have taken a centavo beyond his salary. He was a quiet, thoughtful man, who always dressed in black, and wore a long black cape and high hat. He said little, but when he spoke, people listened.

Years before, after Santa Anna became dictator, Juárez was imprisoned for opposing him. He soon escaped to New Orleans, however, where he made cigars for a living. He returned to Mexico when Santa Anna was displaced by a council of generals and was named Minister of Justice. His new laws provided for the sale of church property not used for worship and restricted the political power of the Catholic Church. Soon the church sympathizers revolted and civil war broke out. Juárez and his companions were hunted from town to town and many people were killed. It was at this point that his opponents imported Emperor Maximilian and the troops of Napoleon.

For several years, Juárez lived near the northern border of Mexico, going from place to place in his black carriage. In the resistance to the French, it was he who held out and finally defeated Maximilian. Before the Emperor was executed, Benito Juárez said, "It is not I, but the people of Mexico, who demand the death of Maximilian."

After the war with the French, Juárez undertook many reforms. He started schools to educate Indian children and reduced the size of the army. This angered the officers who tried to start revolts. Juárez also met resistance from the church. He was so opposed by powerful landowners that he was unable to give out much land to the people who needed it. . . .

Even though Juárez had little time to carry out his plans for his country—he died shortly after he was re-elected to the presidency in 1871—he was greatly loved and mourned.

Reprinted with the permission of Farrar, Straus & Giroux, Inc. from *The Mexican Story*, pp. 56–57, by May McNeer. Copyright 1953 by May McNeer Ward and Lynd Ward.

Do you think that Juárez's early years influenced his later political actions? If so, in what ways? What do his political struggles suggest about the political forces in Mexico in the 1800's? In other countries of Latin America?

Based on the information in the chapter, do you think Juárez was typical of politicians in the 1800's? Why or why not?

How did the army affect Juárez's career?

Do you think that Juárez was typical of most *caudillos* of that time? Explain your answer.

Review

conservatives	*caudillo*	Antonio Guzmán Blanco
liberals	Rafael Trujillo	Benito Juárez
the military	General José Monagas	

10

What was Fidel Castro's role in Latin America?

How effective a political force is communism in
Latin America today?

The Marxist Way

What did the Revolution find when it came to power in Cuba? First of all, it found that 600,000 able Cubans did not have work. That was our permanent unemployment. Three million out of a population of a little over six million did not have electric lights and did not enjoy the advantages and comforts of electricity. Three and a half million out of a total of more than six million lived in huts, shacks, and slums, without any sanitary facilities. In the cities, rents took almost one-third of family incomes. Electricity rates and rents were among the highest in the world. Thirty-seven and one half percent of our people could not read or write; seventy percent of the rural children had no teachers. Ninety-five percent of the children in rural areas had parasites; the infant death rate was very high, the average life span very low.

On the other hand, eighty-five percent of the small farmers were paying rents which came to almost thirty percent of their income for the use of land, while one and one-half percent of the landowners controlled forty-six percent of the total land area of the country. The proportion of hospital beds to the number of people of the country was ridiculous.

In 1959, Fidel Castro created the first Marxist nation in the Western Hemisphere. In 1960, he gave a four and one-half hour speech before the General Assembly of the United Nations. In the part of that speech noted above, he told what life was like for some Cubans at the time of his Revolution. Castro promised the Cubans much-needed reforms, rural health programs, and government housing for the poor. Still, the Cuban people did not want a Communist Revolution. What many of them did want was the overthrow of dictator Fulgencio Batista. At the time, Fidel Castro was their only alternative.

Adapted from Martin Kenner and James Petras (eds.), *Fidel Castro Speaks*, p. 7. Reprinted by permission of Grove Press, Inc. Copyright © 1969 by Martin Kenner and James Petras.

Conditions south of the Rio Grande have been ripe for the Communists for a long time. The poor are tired of their lives of poverty. This alone usually gives the Communists a chance to make headway. Yet the Latin American Communist movement has not met with very much success, even among the people of the lower class. One of the reasons that few gains have been made with this group is that the non-Communist reform parties are so strong. These parties have called for far-reaching reforms and, for this reason, have gained the loyalty of the poor in most of Latin America. The Communists have not had much luck with the peasants either. The little influence they do have in organized labor is not due to the workers' desire to become Marxists. It is mainly because the Communist labor leaders stress "bread and butter" issues such as pay and working conditions.

What conditions in Latin America would seem to make it ready for the Communists to move in?

What has kept the Communists from being very successful in Latin America?

Salvador Allende is shown at a rally in 1971, celebrating his first anniversary as president of Chile. His rule lasted until 1973.

United Press International

The Socialism of Salvador Allende . . . Three Latin American countries—Chile, Cuba, and Guatemala—have come under Marxist influence. Jacobo Arbenz was the president of Guatemala from 1950 to

1954. While he may not have been a Marxist, he was in favor of them. Arbenz was defeated, though, before he had a chance to make long-lasting changes in Guatemala.

Salvador Allende, a Socialist, ruled as president of Chile from 1970 to 1973. He was supported by the Socialists, the Communists, and other such groups. Their support made Allende the only Marxist to come to power through a free, democratic election. During his years in office, Allende made many changes in Chile. Acting with the support of the Chilean Congress, he put all the copper companies under the control of the government. He also bought government control of most of the private banks. He tried to improve the condition of the poor. Milk was given out, and medical care was improved. Wages were increased, and more jobs were created. Allende also began an agrarian reform program to help the poor farmers.

Allende's changes did not please Chile's upper and middle classes. They were afraid that he would take away all of their property. They also feared that democracy might be destroyed. As a result, they began a series of strikes. In 1972, truckers blocked Santiago, the capital. They were upset by reports that the government was going to bring their jobs under State control. Other middle-class Chileans stopped working, and the city's supplies shrank. Violence broke out when a radio station, ignoring what the government said, broadcast critical speeches. One visitor describes what happened below:

> They were leaving Santiago now, those scores of foreign newsmen who had come to Chile to cover a civil war. I watched from the lobby of the Carrera Sheraton Hotel as they piled into taxis and roared off toward Pudahuel International Airport through the city's calm streets.
>
> Only days before, those streets had echoed to the shouts of demonstrators and the muffled crack of police tear-gas canisters. Strikes and riots raged through most of October 1972, as Chile's middle class protested programs of the Government of Popular Unity. . . .
>
> The strikes and riots were acts of desperation launched mainly by the middle class. For the first time in this century, civil war loomed . . . close. Yet, that time, only rocks, tear gas, and [words] flew. Eight months later, there would be bullets.

Finally, in September of 1973, the Chilean army, frightened by Allende's programs for Chile, overthrew the government. A military dictatorship took its place.

What changes did Allende make in Chile? Why did these changes upset the middle and upper classes?

Gordon Young, "Chile: Republic on a Shoestring," *National Geographic,*
Vol. 144, No. 4 (October 1973), p. 437.

Fidel Castro has ruled Cuba since 1959. Some people consider him to be a modern *caudillo*. Castro has tried to improve education, housing, and health care.

Fidel's Cuba . . . The only Marxist government in Latin America to last a long time is that of Fidel Castro, who took power in 1959. Once in power, Castro rapidly led Cuba to socialism, building close ties with the Soviet Union.

Castro has made many changes in Cuba. Education is free for everyone, and illiteracy has all but disappeared. There are many hospitals and clinics, and all medical care is free. Large numbers of public housing units have been built, and the rent in these units is very cheap. Castro also seized farmland. Instead of dividing this land into small farms, he turned it into government-run cooperatives. Through all of this, Castro has ruled Cuba as a dictator. Despite this fact, most foreign observers believe that he enjoys the support of most of the Cuban people. One observer explains:

> For the poor of Latin America, Cuba offers a dignity. This dignity is composed of the rights Cubans have gained under their Communist Revolution. They have the right to a decent job and to wages that will cover their basic needs. They have the right to an equal share of rationed food and clothing and cheap housing. They have the right to free health care and free education for themselves and their children. These rights have been extended to almost everyone, including those who cannot work, blacks, and women.
>
> Those who would argue against this dignity are likely to be the middle class or the wealthy who take basic economic rights for granted. They would cite the need for the right to freedom of speech, assembly, press, religion, and so on. These rights, however, understandably loved by those for whom basic economic rights are no problem, must be listed as secondary. A starving person doesn't worry about freedom of speech.

Adapted from *Inside Cuba*, pp. 223–224, by Joe Nicholson, Jr., Copyright, 1974, Sheed and Ward, Inc.

Even with all the changes Castro has brought to Cuba, the island has serious economic problems. It still depends on the export of farm products, for the most part sugar. Cuba needs the money from exports to buy many of the products the people need. Yet the prices of these exports are often too low in the world market. Then, too, Castro has made some serious economic mistakes. During the early 1960's, he tried to make Cuba an industrialized nation. But the island did not have enough mineral resources, and the people could not provide a large enough market for the industries. Also, it cost a great deal of money to bring in the machinery needed for the factories. As a result, Castro had to drop his plans.

Castro also tried to create a moneyless economy in Cuba. All the people would still do their jobs, but not for wages. Instead, the workers would be rewarded with the goods and other things they needed. This plan did not work, and Castro had to give it up in the early 1970's. The Cuban economy was also hurt by the United States, which tried to keep other

mayo CALENDARIO DE VENTAS

LUNES 3	C1 y C2	TRABAJADORAS
MARTES 4	C2	
MIERCOLES 5	C1	
JUEVES 6	C3 y C4	TRABAJADORAS
VIERNES 7	C4	
SABADO 8	C3	
LUNES 10	D1 y D2	TRABAJADORAS
MARTES 11	D2	
MIERCOLES 12	D1	
JUEVES 13	D3 y D4	TRABAJADORAS

Below: In Cuba, demand is often greater than supply, and waiting in long lines is common. *Flogar* is one of Havana's largest department stores. **Left:** Monthly calendars state who may buy which items and when.

nations from trading with Cuba. Castro had to rely on the Soviet Union for money.

For the Cubans, all of this has brought about the situation described below.

> The physical changes on the island are few, and there are no signs of rising prosperity. . . . Slogans and waiting lines remain the two dominant features of daily life.
>
> Slogans provide guidance to everyone, young and old. On an apartment house: "Our children do not tremble at the threats of imperialist atomic bombs." A highway sign: "People's power—that is really power." . . .
>
> People complain bitterly about being forced to stand in line for buses, for a table at a restaurant, for a seat in a theater, even for a cup of coffee. Says a worker who had been waiting for a bus almost an hour: "We wait and wait for everything—everywhere. But anyone with special privileges can step ahead of us, and there is nothing we can do."
>
> Villages and towns . . . look shabbier than ever before. The old part of Havana appears almost abandoned, although the city's total population has climbed. . . . The shops are half empty. The streets are badly lighted and gloomy. . . .
>
> Cuban women look dowdy in clothes that they must wear year after year because imported cloth is scarce and rations have been reduced. . . .
>
> Some new housing is being built, but not enough to make a dent in the severe shortage. . . .
>
> Basic food is rationed . . . and Government subsidies keep prices at 1962 levels. Housing rents are set at 6 per cent of the head of household's income; utilities and other fixed costs are also minimal.

Carl J. Migdail, "Eyewitness Account of Life in Castro's Cuba." Reprinted from *U.S. News & World Report* (March 28, 1977), pp. 29–30. Copyright 1977 U.S. News and World Report, Inc.

Food and clothing are tightly rationed in Cuba. Cuban citizens must allow enough time to have ration books stamped before buying even the most necessary items.

Rene Burri for Magnum

. . . Banks pay no interest . . . and consumer goods are scarce. The result: a dining-out craze to unload hard-to-spend cash and to escape the dull, repetitious diet of rationed food.

People line up for hours outside restaurants or neighborhood cafes for a meal that offers some variety. Unlike the low-priced rations, however, a restaurant meal can be expensive—up to $15 a person.

. . . A Cuban . . . is entitled to four packs of cigarettes a month at 20 cents each. Above that ration, additional packs cost $1.60 each. Similarly, car owners buy 20 gallons a month of rationed gasoline at 60 cents a gallon. Additional supplies are available at $2 a gallon.

The shortages, rationing and long lines dishearten many Cubans who have worked hard for the revolution but seem to be going nowhere.

Fred Ward for Black Star

The Cuban government allows church weddings. But it requires a civil ceremony. The *Palace of Matrimony* offers free state weddings.

Why do you think that a majority of the Cuban people might support Castro? What social classes would be the least willing to support him? Why? In your opinion, why did so many Cubans flee to the United States when Castro came into power? From what social classes to you think these people came? Why?

Why might the poor value economic improvements above democracy? Are such improvements more important to you than democracy? Explain why or why not.

LA ACTITUD COMUNISTA ANTE LA VIDA ES MOSTRAR CON EJEMPLOS EL CAMINO A SEGUIR.

"Che" . . . Guerrilla movements usually are a form of protest used to correct real or imagined wrongs caused by a foreign invader or ruler. The men and women who become guerrillas or part of a guerrilla movement are, for the most part, volunteers who believe in a cause or a leader. In Latin America, there have been quite a few such movements, but only Fidel Castro's in Cuba was a success. According to many, at the heart of that success was Ernesto "Che" Guevara. "Che" stayed with the Castro government until 1964, when he left Cuba to carry his dreams of revolution to other parts of the world. In 1966, he tried to lead a guerrilla movement in Bolivia. The following reading concerns that campaign.

Guevara apparently crossed the border . . . and made his way to La Paz, where he stayed at the downtown Copacabana Hotel, right on the capital's main street. Like any other tourist, Guevara, a camera bug, took pictures of local scenes and buildings. He also rode around the countryside in a jeep, studying the land and deciding where to begin his operations. He was still in disguise and he wore a jaunty hat, and he had a driver to handle the jeep.

A farm had been purchased in an isolated area. . . . This would be Guevara's base camp, and it was here that he began to train the recruits that were brought in. . . .

Why had Guevara chosen Bolivia to be his target? The conditions in that country must have seemed ideal to him. There were the vast jungle areas in which guerrilla units could incubate, grow, and spread out, eventually to adjoining countries. The Bolivian army consists mainly of one-year recruits—and the army has never won a war, but has lost two. . . . In 142 years of independence, Bolivia has had 55 different administrations. . . .

So there was Bolivia, . . . located in the heartland of South America, and if Guevara could establish a secure base . . . , the . . . movement could be extended into Brazil, Argentina, Peru, Chile, and Paraguay. Guevara had once written, "The war will be continental. . . . There will be many fronts, it will cost much blood. . . ."

On March 23 the guerrillas staged their first ambush. . . .

This . . . was a success, and so were others that followed. As a result of . . . attacks by the rebels, the army casualty toll . . . mounted. . . .

Bolivian army intelligence officers estimate that the guerrillas at their peak numbered about 150 men. There was no certainty, because it was not known how many guerrillas may have deserted. With Guevara were at least 15 Cubans. . . . Among these were four former members of the Central Committee of the Cuban Communist Party, one former vice-minister, and a former director of mines. . . .

After their initial successes, the guerrillas began to suffer setbacks. . . .

. . . They were running short of food, the local peasantry was providing little or no support, and the army was. . . . closing in. Guevara, writing in his diary at the end of September, noted:

So, without doubt, this was the worst month we have had in what there is of this war. The loss of all the caves with a great quantity of documents, medicines, equipment, was a hard blow. This time the army has hit us plenty. The loss of the three best men toward the end of the month, on the 26th, marks a period of decline among the guerrillas. . . .

On October 8, in mid-morning, the troops caught up with Guevara and his small group. An intense firefight developed. . . .

Guevara fought for two hours. Then a bullet hit his M-1 rifle and ricocheted into his left thigh. Guevara surrendered, gasping . . . : "Stop! I'm Che! I'm worth more to you alive than dead." . . .

Placed on a blanket, he was carried by four soldiers to a schoolhouse . . . some two miles distant. There he was [questioned] by Bolivian officers. . . . He pipe-smoked one cigarette after another.

Guevara spoke little. An officer asked him what he was thinking. Guevara did not reply, barely moving his head.

A second officer came up and asked what was the matter. . . .

Slowly, in a low voice, Guevara said, ". . . I'm thinking of the immortality of the revolution."

Guevara, however, was not immortal. A little less than twenty-four hours later an order was received, and at 1:15 P.M. Ernesto Guevara was executed.

Excerpts from "'Che' Guevara: Some Documentary Puzzles at the End of a Long Journey," by Jay Mallin are reprinted from *Journal of Interamerican Studies*, Vol. 10, No. 1 (January 1968), pp. 74–84 by permission of the Publisher, Sage Publishers, Inc.

Why does the author think "Che" chose Bolivia for his revolution? What problems did he find there? Which of these might have to be faced by any guerrilla movement in Latin America? Why?

Since "Che's" death, most guerrilla movements in Latin America have been weakened or wiped out. Do you think the fact that "Che" failed in Bolivia has any bearing on this fact? Why or why not?

What do you think "Che" meant by "the immortality of the revolution"? What does this tell you about his political beliefs?

How do you think the lack of success of the guerrilla movements in Latin America affects the Communist movement in Latin America?

EXPLORATION

Guatemala was one of the towns taken over from its original owners after the 1959 Cuban Revolution. The following article describes the changes the takeover brought to the lives of some people in this sugar mill town once owned by the United Fruit Company.

. . . I went over to the [Communist] Party headquarters. It was closed, and I waited with a 52-year-old woman named Luisa Durán. . . .

"Listen, I have been here before," she said, "and I have been to the administration office [many] times. I wish Fidel [Castro] would come here, I would tell him. I am not afraid, for I do not lie. I am . . . an old revolutionary, a Communist of the old Socialist party, and I tell you it is a shame what they have done to my old man. . . ."

"But that is just our problem," said the Party Secretary, "that we need houses for everyone and that it takes time. Now at least we can say that everyone has hygienic conditions."

"Hygienic?" she said, and gave him a disgusted look. "You want to see the house I have lived in for 26 years? . . ."

"All I can tell you is the Revolution does not care for us old folks," said Luisa. "My old man is retired three years with a miserable $38 a month when he worked all his life. . . ."

"So it comes down to the fact that you want to move to a better house," he said. "But people who are in worse conditions get [first choice], you know that."

"You know who gets the houses," she said. . . .

"It is true that we have to give the technicians some of the new houses," he said. . . .

"They are people who live in their own homes in Havana, and we want them to come here with their special knowledge. We cannot offer them the worst we have!"

"Where do you live?" Luisa asked, with narrowed eyes.

It turned out that the Party Secretary lived in the emergency prefabs built for people who had lost their homes in Hurricane Flora in 1963. . . .

"Then you must know those houses are no good," she said. "I would not live there."

"You would not live there!" said the Party Secretary. "You must have had privileges in the old days. You say you had no trouble getting treated at the hospital—what about the people from the country who did not have the kind of relationship you had with Dr. Ortega that got you that privilege?"

"Listen, I do not lie," said Luisa. " . . . Dr. Ortega never failed to treat me or to give me medicine when a ship had not come in."

"And how long were the periods when ships did not come for sugar and there was no work for stevedores like your husband?"

"There was one time when a ship did not come in for three months and 20 days," Luisa said. "But Dr. Ortega and Raspail at the grocery treated me well. Raspail gave us credit; now, if you do not have 20 cents you get nothing."

"I do not ask you to lie," said the Party man. "I ask you to say that campesinos could not get credit you did or treatment at the hospital."

"What if I told you that the campesinos always got treated free at the hospital?" said Luisa.

The Party man colored and got angry for the first time. "I will tell you about my sister. We brought her on our backs in a hammock because she was so sick we thought she was dying and because there was no ambulance, nothing at all with which to bring her across country. And when we got to the hospital, your Dr. Ortega . . . said, lay her down there, we cannot admit her unless you pay $175 now! And we ran around like madmen borrowing the money."

"But she got treated?"

"Yes, and we sold every animal we had to pay for it." . . .

"I told the Party official right to his face," Luisa said to Mirda, [her] daughter who taught. "We have been treated very bad."

I asked Mirda if she felt the way her mother did. She was wary and said no. I asked if she liked the Revolution. She said yes. "I have not had the experiences my mother has, and I like this. It is what I know."

Luisa looked away from her and said to me, "Old Socialists to them are people to hold tight in their fists."

"Well, Mother, it is your present stance that counts," Mirda said. "Not what you were."

"You are very fresh, Mirda," her mother said. "Some day you will grow old and not count in production."

"And when I do, they should throw me aside."

Jose Yglesias, "How Life Has Changed In a Cuban Sugar Mill Town," *The New York Times Magazine,* July 23, 1967, pp. 88–92. © 1967 by The New York Times Company. Reprinted by permission.

What issues of conflict and resentment appear in the conversation between the Party Secretary and Luisa Durán? How do you account for their differences in attitude?

How does Mirda, Luisa's daughter, feel about the Revolution and its effects? Why do you think her views are so different from her mother's? Does Mirda's attitude suggest anything about the type of influence communism can have on the younger generation? If so, what?

What does the reading suggest about the people's attitude toward Castro?

Based on the information in this chapter, do you feel that the Cuban Revolution was a success or a failure? Explain. In your opinion, will other Latin American nations want to follow Cuba's example in the future? Why or why not?

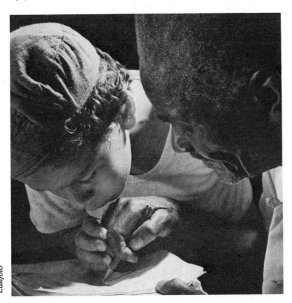

The Castro government has tried to increase the literacy rate. School children are expected to teach their elders who do not read and write how to do so.

Medical care in Cuba is free. The government provides facilities such as this heart disease clinic in Havana.

Review

Marxist	Chilean socialism	Cuban life styles
Communists	Fidel Castro	"Che" Guevara
Salvador Allende	Cuban economy	guerrilla movements

11

Who and what influence reform in
Latin America today?

What is the role of industrialization
in Latin America today?

The New Politics:
A Time for Change

Latin America is in a state of constant change. There is a move to become more modern, to make reforms, to develop. There is, for many, a need to progress and to change. This need has become a part of almost every phase of Latin American life. The following incident took place more than ten years ago. Since then, there have been many more like it. Such incidents are just a small part of what is going on in most Latin American nations today.

"The only thing the Mayor gives us is lead in our bodies," an occupant of a large squatter settlement in central Bogotá [Colombia] said today.

Alonso Valbuena, a 35-year-old hospital orderly who is working as a teacher, was stretched out on a cot in his squalid hut of tin and cardboard. His leg was in a cast from two bullet wounds and he displayed the bruises received last week during a battle with the police.

The clash left two children and one adult dead and about 100 injured, including 17 police officers. Seventy civilians were jailed by the police.

Mr. Valbuena is one of 8,000 people who have lived for the last five years in a shantytown called Policarpa Salavarrienta.

The land is owned by the National University, which plans to build a medical center on it. Last Friday 300 migrants arrived from other parts of town and put up shacks on a ballfield next to the land.

About two hours later a 300-man police block was drawn around the area. An officer announced on a loudspeaker that everyone must leave in 10 minutes.

The warning was not heeded. Instead, a loudspeaker from the center announced, "We are prepared to defend our homes with our lives!"

The fight lasted more than two hours. The police then tore down the shacks and removed broken furniture, pots, religious pictures and other debris from the ballfield.

Adapted from "Squatter Inroads Fought by Bogota: Police Tear Down Shacks in Center of City," *The New York Times,* April 13, 1966, Sec. L, p. 15. © 1966 by The New York Times Company. Reprinted by permission.

BACKGROUND

By the end of the 1800's, Latin Americans wanted a change. They felt that the time had come to modernize. Foreign money was used to expand the transportation and communication systems. Factories and commercial farms were developed, and the cities were made more modern. More Europeans came to settle in Latin America. Because of all this, some Latin Americans set out to destroy the old-style politics of their countries. They felt that until this was done, the needed social and economic changes could not happen. Labor began to organize, and the middle class began to push its way into the politics of a number of Latin American countries. The middle-class groups worked to make sure there were free elections. In return for the support the workers gave them, they passed the first social welfare laws. That was just the beginning.

Providing adequate housing for the people is still a major problem in many areas of Latin America.

Robert Hatton

Today the desire for social change dominates Latin American politics. The few old, conservative parties that are still active are not strong, and their leaders see the new groups as threats. Many of the older parties are against the reforms, which they fear will hurt their profits and social positions. One Latin American country that cares a great deal about reform and social change is Mexico. From 1969 to 1975, the president of Mexico was Don Luis Echeverría. According to one report:

> Don Luis tried to be a master builder, both for the *campesinos*—the landless peasants of Mexico—and for the country's new middle classes. He sank at least $100 million in . . . the new resort areas of Cancún and Ixtapa. He also built a steel mill and hydroelectric plants and financed new oil exploration—all worthy projects but ill timed in the midst of worldwide recession.

"The Road Back to Confidence," *Time*, February 21, 1977, p. 34. Reprinted by permission from *Time*, The Weekly News Magazine; Copyright Time Inc. 1977.

Echeverría was succeeded by José López Portillo, who continued with Echeverría's plans. López Portillo's plans for Mexico are reported below:

López Portillo had no opposition. He ranged from Tijuana in the north to Tapachula in the south, covering 40,600 miles in the course of nine months, traveling at times by horse, and by bus and plane. He did very little preaching, but he called for an "alliance for production" between business and government to come up with 300,000 new jobs.

In his first days in office, he kept a low profile and spent most of his time on restoring confidence and attacking Mexico's economic crisis. In December he got 140 companies to join the alliance for production and step up investments. Mexican businessmen responded with full-page newspaper advertisements promising they would help.

López Portillo, in an interview at his office, said that the primary problems of the government are "food, energy, education, health, unemployment and inflation. But our first goal is . . . that of feeding our people and [making sure that] all of them have at least the minimum level of welfare."

His views on other topics:

On land distribution: "There has been too much faith placed in the redistribution of land as a means of solving inequalities. The truth is that this is no longer a real possibility for the more than 1.5 million peasants who still have no land. What the peasant really seeks is job and income security. There are other ways of offering that."

On tax reform and redistribution of wealth: "We will look for ways of improving our tax laws. They must not only satisfy the need to bring in more government income and regulate economic activity; tax rates must also be more in line with what a person is able to pay."

Before he took office, López Portillo coined the catch phrase *la solución somos todos* (the solution is all of us). He might have been thinking about a passage from his own book, *Quetzalcoatl:*

". . . Do not doubt. Keep up your conviction to serve! And remember that there is more merit in using your force for the benefit of the suffering than for your own gain!"

Rich Brommer

What led to political reform in Latin America? What were some of the results?

Do you think that López Portillo is a reform politician? Why or why not? Do you think his campaign and the programs he wants would have been accepted a hundred years ago? Why or why not?

Ibid., adapted from pp. 35–36.

The State of Development . . . Most Latin American nations have been trying to bring about industrial growth since World War II. Yet because modern industry has come late, Latin America is thought of as underdeveloped. Many Latin Americans think that industrial development will take care of most of their problems. They feel that it will provide jobs for the rapidly growing population and bring better pay for the lower-income groups. They hope it will promote more wealth for those in business. They see it as the way to make Latin Americans self-sufficient. For them, it is the road to the higher standard of living most Latin Americans desire.

There have been great increases in the last few years in the production of electrical energy, steel, cars, oil, cement, paper, and many other products. But this has not been enough to meet the needs of the growing numbers of Latin Americans. Between 70 and 75 percent of the needed manufactured goods still must be imported. Even in areas with a lot of industry, such as São Paulo, Brazil, and Mexico City, the standard of living still is low.

Industrialization in Latin America has increased since World War II. Right: A worker loads iron bars at a metal company in Peru. Below: This cement factory in San Salvador has given a boost to its economy.

David Mangurian

John Pennington/The Picture Cube

There are many reasons why the industry in Latin America has not grown as fast as some would like. There is not enough money or skilled labor. There are too few transportation systems. Then, too, most Latin

Americans just do not have enough purchasing power yet to support rapid industrial expansion.

One Latin American country which is using its own resources to create new industry and stand on its own is Brazil. Its main industries at present are iron and steel, metalworking, textiles, and food processing. But Brazilians are branching out, as seen in the reading which follows.

> Brazil continues to press its plans to become a superpower. With its population of 112 million people, a strong industrial base and a great amount of natural resources, Brazil should move fast toward that goal.
>
> This country is No. 1 in world coffee production, second in soybeans, third in manganese and eighth in tin, motor vehicles and shipbuilding.
>
> The outlook is impressive. Projections show that Brazil's iron-ore exports, second only to Australia's, will soar to 141 million tons by 1985. That will be enough to make Brazil the world leader.
>
> Already the world's sixteenth largest steel producer, Brazil counts on a 20-billion-dollar expansion program to raise production from 9.2 million tons in 1976 to 28 million tons by 1985.
>
> Barely touched deposits of bauxite, used in making aluminum, may produce 9 million tons a year by 1985. This could go higher if reserves in the Amazon jungles are tapped.
>
> Brazil has also become an agricultural giant, second only to the United States this year [1977] as an exporter of farm products. Some of Brazil's biggest development projects are aimed at making the country less dependent on oil from other countries.
>
> State-controlled Petrobras has signed contracts with four outside firms to look for offshore oil and gas.
>
> The first of several planned nuclear power plants is to be ready by the end of 1978. The first plant is being built by Westinghouse and Brazilian contractors on the Atlantic Coast between Rio de Janeiro and São Paulo.
>
> Construction is under way on the largest hydroelectric project in the world. The first unit of the 6-billion-dollar, 12.5-million-kilowatt dam and power plant west of São Paulo is due to begin operation by early 1983.

Why do some people feel that Latin America is underdeveloped? Do you agree with them? Why or why not?

Why do many Latin Americans feel that it is important to develop industry?

Do you think that other Latin American countries could industrialize as Brazil has? Why or why not? What has Brazil accomplished with its industrial growth? What do you think this growth might do to the way of life of the Brazilians?

Adapted from a copyrighted article "Why Angry Brazil Shaped Up as Rosalynn's Toughest Challenge," in *U.S. News & World Report*, June 13, 1977, pp. 44–45.

Pressure Groups . . . The struggle for change in Latin America involves pressure groups. Some of these groups want change; some oppose it; and some are undecided. One of these groups is the Catholic Church, which favors reform in Latin America. In some countries, like Mexico, Chile, Colombia, Argentina, and Peru, the Church still has a great deal of influence. In others, like Nicaragua, Paraguay, and Bolivia, the Church has almost no say at all.

Another pressure group is made up of the owners of great estates. Although politically these landowners still dominate some rural areas, most of their power comes only after they have joined with other groups. In some cases, they will agree to help another group who, in turn, will do something for them. For example, reform groups will promise to leave the estates alone if the landowners will back reform laws that treat only city problems. In some countries, such as Peru, Cuba, and Bolivia, the landowners have lost their lands and their political power. But, in others, they have been able to resist agrarian reform and taxes. They also have been able to stop farm workers from forming unions.

The most effective lower-class pressure group is organized labor. For the most part, this group is under government control and short of money. Because of this, its chances of winning strikes are not good. It is simpler for labor to gain its financial aims through politics than through strikes. But as this group does not include most city workers, a large part of the working class does not share in its political or economic gains. Most urban areas do have managerial pressure groups. These groups are a force for economic development in all of Latin America except Cuba and Brazil. They are against agrarian reform, which they see as an attack on private property. At the same time, often they are against higher pay for the lower class. Most feel that pay increases are a threat to their cheap labor supply.

Still another important pressure group is college students. Students are very much a part of Latin American politics. The experience gained while still in school is thought to be a good base for a later career in politics. Most student leaders are eager to become a part of national affairs while still in school. Most have a strong desire for change and feel that the way to bring about that change is by direct action. Many of the students are influenced by communism. Although most are not Communists, they are willing to work with those who are.

But by far the most powerful pressure group is the army, which has the deciding voice in almost every Latin American nation. In the past, the army stepped in to further the ambitions of a *caudillo* or to keep the country the way the landowners wanted it. Today's army officers, for the most part, are a different breed. Most favor economic development. Some support social reforms. Still, most show little concern for democracy. In most cases, when the army steps in, it is for different reasons than in the past. One country under military rule is Peru, where in 1968 the army came in and threw out President Fernando Belaunde Terry. The military government that took over the country said that it did so because the political leaders did not care about the needs of most of the people. What followed in Peru is noted below.

The new government said it would end the political and economic control of Peru by the "top 40 families" and foreign corporations through a program of "social democracy." They said it would guide the nation on a path between capitalism and communism.

In the "Inca Plan," a blend of public and private sectors of the economy was called for. The first phase—which the government says was largely completed by 1975—called for heavy state involvement in basic industries. So the government took most communications firms and banks. Under the Plan, workers will slowly gain co-ownership of most industries.

At the heart of the program is land reform, one of the largest found in Latin America. Before, fully 90 percent of all farmland was controlled by just 2 percent of the people. The government hopes to change this by dealing out 25 million acres to worker-owned cooperatives and to families.

This kind of strong policy will help build the "new Peruvian man," the generals say. To speed things up, the government has expanded educational programs, increased incomes, and promised to spend new oil earnings on social programs. It has turned over factories and farms to workers.

Oddly, these reforms, started in the name of "the people," have not made the government more popular. One reason is that the generals run Peru like an army barracks. Congress is done away with, and political parties are made to obey or made to leave the country. Only soldiers can be in the cabinet. Professional groups and free labor unions are jailed (or made to leave the country). Having taken over the broadcast media in 1971, the generals took over the major newspapers and magazines in 1974.

What is the role of the pressure groups in Latin America? Who makes up the membership of these groups? Why are they so important?

Why, in your opinion, is the army so strong in Latin America today? What happened in Peru when the military took control? Why have the reforms they made in Peru not made the government more popular with the people? How would you feel toward the government if you were a Peruvian?

Adapted from Jon D. Cozean, *Latin America* (Washington, D.C.: Stryker-Post Publications, 1975), p. 90.

A Move Toward Nationalism . . .

In recent years, Latin Americans have begun to care more and more about the interests of their nations. As this sense of nationalism grows, so does the desire to be rid of outside political and economic influences. Many Latin Americans want independent foreign policy based on what is best for their countries. They want the same for their economies. This has led many Latin Americans to resent foreign investors. Among the many countries that have invested in Latin America is the United States. Mexican author Carlos Fuentes is one of the many Latin Americans who do not like the foreign influences. In the account which follows, Fuentes lashes out against the United States for its part in the economy of Latin America.

One of the basic factors of backwardness in Latin America is the economic change that comes from foreign control of our economies. Ah, you jump at this point. You refuse to admit this. You have helped the development (what development?) of Latin America. You unselfishly give us dollars and technical aid.

There is the control of natural resources: iron ore, copper, tin, coal, lead, zinc, oil. These resources, in your hands, enter your economy: they are not used in the internal development of our countries.

You are also masters of Latin American foreign trade. Sixty percent of that trade is with you, according to the prices you set. American companies manage 75 percent of our commercial movement. You set the conditions and the prices.

Ask the great cotton concerns how much they pay for a bale of Mexican cotton. Then ask at what price they sell it to the English in Hong Kong, and how much they charge the Communist government of China for it. Anderson Clayton [a large American company in Brazil] makes five times the amount in this operation than the Mexican grower does.

Investments? Yes, you have invested billions of dollars in Latin America. It is a curious thing: we have always received your investments, and we are still poor. You speak about *your* property in Latin America and call us thieves when we take it away. But why don't you ask your investors? Ask them how much they invest and how much they take back to the United States in profits. You take out too much, leave too little, and even this little is distributed unfairly. Where is the real benefit for our economies? Is it just that these profits do nothing, not a single thing, to ease the horrible misery, ignorance, and illness of the Latin Americans who, with their slavery, made them possible? You, as Americans, tell me if that is just.

And tell me also whether you have not recovered more than your investments. Tell me whether it is not right that this lost wealth should be recovered and used to improve the lot of everyone though today it benefits only a dozen corporations.

Adapted from Carlos Fuentes, "The Argument of Latin America," *Whither Latin America?*, pp. 14–16. Copyright © 1963 by Monthly Review Inc. Reprinted by permission of Monthly Review Press.

How does Fuentes show his nationalism? Why does he blame the United States for some of Latin America's economic problems?

Why, if at all, would other Latin Americans agree with Fuentes' strong criticism of North American business operations in Latin America? What arguments could be made against the author's stand?

A Chilean economist made the following statement about foreign investments in Chile: "Our idea is that if foreign investment contributes no more than capital, we are not interested. We want the foreign firm to bring technology and entry into export markets. We are not interested if a firm is not going to produce for export." Compare and contrast his comments with those made by Fuentes. Are they really saying the same thing? Why or why not?

Do you think the United States should have a role in the Latin American economy? If not, why? If so, what should that role be?

David Mangurian

David Mangurian

Many countries in other parts of the world have made investments in Latin America. Above: This is a French automobile assembly plant in Arica, Chile. Left: A worker rivets an automobile body at an American automobile plant in Mexico City.

THIS IS A SYNTHESIS OF MILITARY POLITICS IN LATIN AMERICA.....

1 IN COUNTRY 'A' GENERALISIMO 'B' RULES-HE IS A DICTATOR

2 COLONEL 'C' REBELS-THE PEOPLE BACK HIM

3 THE REVOLUTION SUCCEEDS

THE DICTATOR 'B' FLEES WITH ALL THE MONEY

4

THE COUNTRY IS BROKE - THEY MUST START ALL OVER

5

6 COLONEL 'C' PROMISES ELECTIONS AND REFORMS...

7 THE ARMY MAKES HIM A GENERAL -

8 PROMISES ARE FORGOTTEN - HE NAMES HIMSELF "GENERALISIMO"

Adapted from the book *The Best of Impossible Worlds* by Abel Quezada. © 1963 by Prentice-Hall, Inc. Published by Prentice-Hall, Inc., Englewood Cliffs, New Jersey.

Do you think that the cartoon accurately shows the role of the military in Latin America today? Explain your answer. Do you think it depicts the military in the 1800's? Explain your answer.

What does the cartoon suggest about the Latin American people and the way they feel about reform? Based on the information in this chapter, do you think that this is a true picture of the modern Latin American attitude toward reform? Explain your answer.

What does the cartoon suggest about the ruler's reasons for taking power? Do you think this is a true picture of recent Latin American heads of state? Explain your answer, based on the information in the chapter.

If the Latin American country in the cartoon had industrialized, do you think the chain of events would have been as shown in the cartoon? Why or why not?

Review

social change
Don Luis Echeverría
José López Portillo

land distribution
political reform
pressure groups

industrialization
nationalism

GLOSSARY

LATIN AMERICA GLOSSARY

adobe: (ah *thoh* bay) sun-dried brick

agrarian reform: attempt to divide land more evenly and to improve the life of the peasants

Allende, Salvador: (Ah *yen* day, Sahl van *thor*) Socialist president of Chile 1970–1973; responsible for improved living conditions

altiplano: (ahl tee *plah* noh) gloomy, cold plains in the mountains of Peru and Bolivia where life is very hard

anticlericalism: movement to limit the power of the Church in social, economic, and political affairs

Araucana: (Ah row *kah* nah) dialect spoken in Chile

Arbenz, Jacobo: (Ahr *bens*, Hah *koh* boh) president of Guatemala 1950–1954

Atacama Desert: (Ah tah *kah* mah) driest region in Latin America, located along the coast of northern Chile

Aymara: (Eye *mah* rah) dialect of Bolivia

Aymaras: (Eye *mah* rahs) Indian people in the mountains of Peru and Bolivia

Aztecs: Indians of central Mexico who developed a highly civilized empire; conquered by the Spanish in the sixteenth century

barriada: (bah ree *ah* thah) shantytown

Batista, Fulgencio: (Bah *tees* tah, Fool *hen* see oh) military leader, dictator, and president of Cuba; overthrown in 1959

Blanco, Antonio Guzmán: (*Blahn* koh, Ahn *toh* nee oh Goos *mahn*) president of Venezuela 1870–1877; responsible for much material development

campesino: (kahm pay *see* noh) peasant farmer

candomblé [also **macumba** and **xangô**]: (kahn dohm *blay*) (mah *koom* bah) (*jahn* goh) magic of Brazilian blacks, much like witchcraft

Carioca: (Kah ree *oh* kah) native of Rio de Janeiro

Carnival: (Kahr nee *vahl*) celebration marking the beginning of the Christian Lenten season

Castro, Fidel: (*Kahs* troh, Fee *thel*) leader of the 1959 Revolution in Cuba, resulting in the first Marxist nation in the Western Hemisphere

caudillo: (kow *thee* yoh) head of a state (or part of it) with power seized through military force; often a dictator

centavo: (sen *tah* voh) hundredth part of the monetary unit in various countries

commercial farm: place which produces goods for sale on the world market

conservatives: those who favor a strong central government with a strong president and weak legislature

cordillera: (kor thee *yay* rah) central range of the Andes Mountains

Cortés, Hernando: (Kor *tays*, Er *nahn* doh) Spanish explorer who conquered the Mexican Aztecs in the sixteenth century

cruzeiro: (kroo *zay* roh) monetary unit of Brazil, 100 *centavos*

Cuauhtémoc: (Kwah *tay* mohk) last Aztec ruler in Mexico

Echeverría, Don Luis: (Ay chay vay *ree* ah, Don Loo *ees*) president of Mexico 1969–1975

ejido: (ay *hee* thoh) small Mexican farm owned by a community of people; given to an individual for personal use or worked collectively

favelas [also **villas miserias, ranchos,** and **tugurios**]: (fah *vay* lahs) (*vee* yahs mee *say* ree ahs) (*rahn* chohs) (too *goo* ree ohs) poor areas or slums in major Latin American cities

fiesta: (fee *yes* tah) festive celebration of a saint's day

gaucho: (*gow* choh) native cowboy in the *pampas* of Argentina

Guaraní: (Gwah rah *nee*) dialect spoken in Paraguay

Guevara, Ernesto "Che": (Gay *vah* rah, Er *nes* toh "Chay") Cuban revolutionist and guerrilla leader in Bolivia

Guzmán, Antonio Leocadio: (Goos *mahn*, Ahn toh nee oh Lay oh *kah* thee oh) journalist in Venezuela; vice-president and minister of the interior under President José Monagas

hacendado: (ah sen *dah* thoh) owner of a landed estate who rules the peasants, telling them when and what to plant

hacienda: (ah *see en* dah) landed estate used for farming or ranching

Inca Plan: (*Een* kah) Peruvian attempt to involve the government in basic industry and in land reform

Incas: (*Een* kahs) Indians of Peru who created a highly developed empire before the Spanish conquest

Juárez, Benito: (*Hwah* res, Bay *nee* toh) president of Mexico 1858–1872, the first Indian ruler since the Aztecs; leader of the reform movement

liberals: those who favor local self-rule; want strong legislature to limit the executive power

llanos: (*yah* nohs) grassy plains in Colombia and Venezuela

machismo [also **hombría**]: (mah *cheez* moh) (ohm *bree* ah) manliness, maleness

Maximilian: emperor of Mexico 1864–1867

Maya: (*Meye* yah) Indian dialect spoken in Bolivia

Mayans: Indians who developed a very early advanced civilization in northern Central America and the Yucatán Peninsula of Mexico

mayordomo: (meye yor *thom* moh) supervisor of a work gang in the sugar cane fields

mestizo: (mes *tee* soh) person of mixed blood; in Latin America, a person of European and American Indian ancestry

minifundia: (mee nee *foon* dee ah) two-to-fifteen- acre farm, common in Latin America

Monagas, José: (Moh *nah* gahs, Hoh *say*) general and president of Venezuela in the middle nineteenth century

mulatto: offspring of one black parent and one white parent

Náhuatl: (*Hah* wahtl) language of the Aztec Indians

Nosso Senhor do Bomfim: (*Noh* soh Sen *yor* do Bohn *feem*) church for blacks in Bahia; mixture of Christian and old African rites

"nouveaux riches": those who have made their fortunes in this century, the newly rich

pampas: (*pahm* pahs) vast grassy plains in Argentina

peso: (*pay* soh) silver and copper coin; monetary unit of certain Latin American countries

Portillo, López: (Por *tee* yoh, *Loh* pes) president of Mexico 1975; advocate of an alliance for production

Quechua: (*Kay* choo ah) Indian dialect spoken in Bolivia and other Latin American countries

Quiche: (*Kee* chay) dialect spoken in Guatemala

Santa Anna: soldier of fortune who became president of Mexico; given the title Dictator; removed in 1855

siesta: (see *yes* tah) afternoon period set aside for resting and sleeping

Tenochtitlán: (Tay nohch tee *tlahn*) Aztec capital of Mexico

Terry, Fernando Belaunde: (*Tay* ree, Fer *nahn* doh Bay lah *oon* day) president of Peru, removed in 1968 by military force

Trujillo, Rafael: (Troo *hee* yoh, Rah fah *el*) dictator of the Dominican Republic 1930–1961

zambo: (*sahm* boh) person of mixed blood, half black and half Indian

INDEX

LATIN AMERICA INDEX

Aconcagua Peak, 5–6
Agrarian reform, 54, 81, 88–89, 107, 122
  Allende, Salvador, 107
  campesinos, 81
  Catholic Church, 54
  labor, 122
  landowners, 122
  peasants, 81, 88–89
Agriculture, 10, 25, 74, 80–91, 107, 121
  agrarian reform, 81, 88–89, 107
  blacks, 25
  Brazil, 121
  campesinos, 81
  commercial farms, 85–87
  haciendas, 83–85
  Japanese, 25
  migrants, 74
  pampas, 10
  peasants, 83–85
  sharecropping, 83, 86
Allende, Salvador, 107
Altiplano, 15
Amazon River, 12–14
Andes, 5–8
Anticlericals, 53
Araucana, 22
Arbenz, Jacobo, 106–107
Argentina, 9–10, 14, 19, 23, 71, 85, 97, 122
  blacks, 19
  Catholic Church, 122
  climate, 14
  commercial farms, 85
  Facundo, 97
  gaucho, 10
  immigrants, 23
  pampas, 9–10
  villas miserias, 71
Aristocracy, 33
Army, 92–103, 122–123
  caudillos, 96–103, 123
  politics, 94–97
  pressure group, 122–123
Asians, 19, 25
Atacama Desert, 14
Aymara, 15, 19, 22
Aztec Indians, 20, 22, 103

Bahia, 56–57
Balance-of-trade, 82
Baseball (*beisbol*), 44

Batista, Fulgencio, 105
Birth control, 73
Blacks, 19, 24–25, 52, 56–57
  Bahia, 56–57
  Catholic Church, 52
Blanco, Antonio Guzmán, 101
Bogotá, 54, 71
Bolivia, 15, 19, 22, 61, 89, 112–113, 122
  agrarian reform, 89
  altiplano, 15
  Aymara, 19
  Catholic Church, 122
  education, 61
  guerrilla movement, 112–113
  Guevara, "Che," 112–113
  Indians, 15, 19, 22
  landowners, 122
  mestizo, 19
Brazil, 9, 12–14, 19, 23–25, 43, 46, 55, 56–57, 71, 85, 120–121, 122
  agriculture, 121
  blacks, 19, 24–25, 56–57
  commercial farms, 85
  Europeans, 23
  favelas, 71
  fiesta, 46
  industry, 120, 121
  Japanese, 25
  labor, 122
  Nosso Senhor do Bomfim, 56–57
  plains, 9
  Portuguese, 19, 23
  Protestants, 55
  rivers and deserts, 12–14
  soccer (*futebol*), 43
Buenos Aires, 9, 24

Campesinos, 81, 118
Candomblé, 56–57
Carácas, 71, 101
Castro, Fidel, 104–105, 108–112
  communism, 104–105
  Communist Revolution, 105, 108
  Cuba, 105, 108–112
  economic problems, 109–111
  guerrilla movement, 112
  Guevara, "Che," 112
  Marxist government, 105, 108
  reforms, 105, 108
  Soviet Union, 108, 110

United States, 109
Catholic Church, 50–58, 73, 95, 103, 122
  agrarian reform, 54
  anticlericals, 53
  birth control, 73
  blacks, 52
  Colombia, 54
  combination of faiths, 56–57
  Indians, 52
  influence in various countries, 122
  Juárez, Benito, 103
  Mexico, 103
  Nosso Senhor do Bomfim, 56–57
  patron saints, 51, 58
  politics, 54, 95
  Pope Paul VI, 54
  Portuguese, 52
  reforms, 53, 122
  Spanish, 52
Cauca-Magdalena River, 12
Caudillos, 96–103, 122
  Argentina, 97
  army, 122
  Blanco, Antonio Guzmán, 101
  Dominican Republic, 98–99
  Facundo, 97
  Juárez, Benito, 102–103
  Mexico, 97, 103
  military leaders, 96–99
  Monagas, José, 100
  politics, 96–99
  Santa Anna, 97
  Trujillo, Rafael, 98–99
  Venezuela, 100–101
Chile, 5, 14, 22, 106–107, 122, 125
  agrarian reforms, 107
  Allende, Salvador, 106–107
  Araucana, 22
  Atacama Desert, 14
  Catholic Church, 122
  changes, 107
  Communists, 106–107
  investments, 125
  Marxist government, 106–107
  Santiago, 5, 107
  Socialists, 107
  strikes, 107
Chinese, 25
Climate, 11, 12, 14, 15
Colombia, 9, 10, 12, 54, 71, 85, 122

Catholic Church, 54, 122
Cauca-Magdalena River, 12
commercial farms, 85
llanos, 9
Orinoco River, 10
Pope Paul VI, 54
tugurios, 71
Combination of faiths, 56–57
Commercial farms, 31, 85–87
Communist Revolution (Cuba), 105, 108
Communists, 104–115, 122
    Allende, Salvador, 106–107
    Bolivia, 112–113
    Castro, Fidel, 104–105, 108, 112
    Chile, 106–107
    Cuba, 104–105, 108–112
    Guatemala, 114–115
    Guevara, "Che," 112–113
    Marxist government, 104–115
    students, 122
Cortés, Hernando, 20–22
Cuba, 25, 104–105, 108–112, 122
    Asians, 25
    Batista, Fulgencio, 105
    Castro, Fidel, 104–105, 108–112
    changes, 105, 108, 109
    Communists, 104–105, 108–112
    economic problems, 109–111
    guerrilla movement, 112
    Guevara, Ernesto "Che," 112
    labor, 122
    landowners, 122
    Marxist government, 105, 108
    Soviet Union, 108, 110
    United States, 109
Culture, 41

Democracy, 93, 95, 122
Dominican Republic, 85, 98, 99
    commercial farms, 85
    Trujillo, Rafael, 98–99
Doña Barbara, 11

Echeverría, Don Luis, 118–119
Economy, 13, 15, 23, 45, 53, 72, 81, 83, 85, 88–89, 109, 119, 122–124
Ecuador, 22, 61, 85
    commercial farms, 85
    education, 61
    Indians, 22
Education, 32, 52, 53, 60–69, 101
    Blanco, Antonio Guzmán, 101

Catholic Church, 52, 53, 64
    courses, 62, 66, 67
    higher education, 67
    Indians, 68
    private schools, 64–65
    public education, 61–63
    vocational schools, 66
Ejido, 86
Europeans, 19, 23, 24, 53
Exports, 82, 85, 109, 121, 125

Facundo, 97
Family, 28–39, 51, 74–75, 78
    Catholic Church, 51
    lower class, 30–32
    middle class, 35–37
    migrants, 74–75, 78
    role of women, 38
    upper class, 33–35
Farming, see *Agriculture*
Favelas, 71
Fiestas, 46–47
Foreign investments, 118, 124
Foreign policy, 124
Fuentes, Carlos, 124

Gallegos, Rómulo, 11
Gaucho, 9–11
Guaraní, 19, 22
Guárico River, 11
Guatemala, 9, 22, 56, 85, 105–107, 114–115
    Arbenz, Jacobo, 106–107
    coastal plains, 9
    combination of faiths, 56
    commercial farms, 85
    Indians, 22
    Marxist government, 105–107
    Quiche, 22
Guerrilla movements, 112–113
Guevara, Ernesto "Che," 112–113
Guzmán, Antonio Leocadio, 101

Haciendas, 31, 83–85, 89
Honduras, 9, 85
Human diversity, 19

Immigrants, 10, 23
Imports, 82, 120
Inca Indians, 15, 20
Inca Lake, 5
Indians, 8, 15, 19–22, 49, 52, 68, 103
    altiplano, 15
    Catholic Church, 52
    culture, 20–22

    education, 68
    Europeans, 22
    Juárez, Benito, 103
    languages, 19, 22
    Tenochtitlán, 20–22
Industry, 13, 14, 35, 73, 109, 120–121
    Amazon River, 13
    Atacama Desert, 14
    birthrate, 73
    Cuba, 109
    development, 120–121
    middle class, 35
Intermarriage, 19, 22

Japanese, 25
Juárez, Benito, 102-103
Juncal River, 5

Labor, 24–25, 106, 118, 122
    Asians, 25
    blacks, 24–25
    changes, 118
    Communists, 106
    pressure group, 122
Landholdings, 53, 83, 85–86
    Catholic Church, 53
    commercial farms, 85
    ejido, 86
    haciendas, 83
    minifundia, 86
Landowners, 33, 122
Languages, 19, 22
Llanos, 9–11
Lower class, 30–32

Machismo, 49, 73
Macumba, 56
Manaus, 13
Maqui, Rosendo, 68
Marriages, 31
Marxist government, 104–115
    Allende, Salvador, 106–107
    Arbenz, Jacobo, 106–107
    Bolivia, 112–113
    Castro, Fidel, 105, 108–112
    Chile, 106–107
    Cuba, 105, 108–112
    Guatemala, 106–107, 114–115
    Guevara, Ernesto "Che," 112–113
Maya Indians, 20, 26
Maximilian, 103
Melgarejo, 93
Mestizo, 19, 22, 97
Mexico, 8, 9, 14, 20, 22, 97, 103, 118–120

campesinos, 118
climate, 14
coastal plains, 9
Cortés, Hernando, 20
Echeverría, Don Luis, 118–119
economy, 119
Indians, 8, 22
industry, 120
Juárez, Benito, 103
Náhuatl, 22
Portillo, José López, 119
reform, 118–119
Santa Anna, 97
Tenochtitlán, 20
Middle class, 29–30, 35–37
Migrants, 31, 74–75, 78
Military, 96–99
Minifundia, 86–87
Monagas, José, 100
Mulatto, 19

Náhuatl, 22
Nationalism, 124
Natural resources, 23, 121
Nicaragua, 9, 85, 122
Nosso Senhor do Bomfim, 56–57
"Nouveaux riches," 33–34

Orinoco River, 10, 12

Pampas, 9–11
Panama, 25
Paraguay, 9, 19, 22, 122
Catholic Church, 122
Guaraní, 19, 22
inland plains, 9
Spanish, 22
Paraná-La Plata, 12
Paron Lake, 7
Patron saints, 51, 58
Peasants, 30–31, 81, 83–85, 88, 106
agrarian reform, 88
campesinos, 81
Communists, 106
haciendas, 83–85
lower class, 30–31
Peru, 8, 14, 15, 19, 22, 25, 61, 122, 123
altiplano, 15
army, 122–123
Asians, 25
Atacama Desert, 14
Catholic Church, 122
education, 61

Indians, 8, 22
Japanese, 25
landowners, 122
mestizo, 19
Quechua, 19
Terry, Fernando Belaunde, 123
Politics, 49, 54–55, 62, 72, 92–103, 118–119, 122–123
army, 94–99
Catholic Church, 54, 95
caudillos, 96–99
education, 62
Juárez, Benito, 103
machismo, 49
population, 72
Portillo, José López, 119
pressure groups, 122–123
social reform, 93, 118–119
Pope Paul VI, 54
Portillo, José López, 119
Portuguese, 19, 22, 23, 52
Pressure groups, 122–123
Protestants, 55

Quetzalcoatl, 119
Quechua, 19, 22
Quiche, 22

Ranchos, 71
Recife, 56
Reform, 53, 54, 81, 88–89, 105–107, 116–127
agrarian reform, 54, 81, 88–89, 107, 122
Catholic Church, 53
development, 120–121
land reform, 53
nationalism, 124
pressure groups, 122–123
social reform, 93, 118, 122–123
Regeneration, 101
Religion, 22, 50–58, 73, 95, 103, 122
Catholic Church, 50–58, 73, 95, 103, 122
combination of faiths, 56–57
Indians, 22
patron saints, 51, 58
Protestants, 55
Retamar, Roberto Fernandez, 41
Rio de Janeiro, 43, 46–47, 56, 71
Rio Grande, 23, 106
Rio Negro, 12
Roles of men and women, 32, 33, 36, 38

Santa Anna, 97, 103
Santiago, 5, 107
Saõ Francisco, 12
Saõ Paulo, 71, 120
Sarmiento, Domingo, 10
Shantytowns, 74–75
Sharecropping, 83, 86
Siesta, 47
Soccer (*futebol*), 43
Social class, 29–30
Socialists, 107
Social reform, 93, 118, 122–123
Soviet Union, 108, 110
Spanish, 19–23, 52
Sports, 43–45
Strikes, 67, 107
Students, 60–67, 122
higher education, 67
pressure groups, 122
private schools, 64–65
public schools, 61–63
vocational schools, 66–67
see also, *Education*

Teachers, see *Students*
Technology, 23, 125
Tenochtitlán, 20–22
Terry, Fernando Belaunde, 123
Trujillo, Rafael, 98–99
Tugurios, 71
Tupengato Peak, 5–6

United Nations, 105
United States, 30, 109, 124
Upper class, 30, 33–34, 107
Urbanization, 73–79
Uruguay, 9, 23, 85

Venezuela, 9, 10, 12, 44, 63, 71, 100, 101
baseball, 44
Blanco, Antonio Guzmán, 101
education, 63
llanos, 9
Monagas, José, 100
Orinoco River, 10, 12
ranchos, 71
Villas miserias, 71

Xangô, 56

Yucatán Peninsula, 9

Zambo, 19